Beneath
White Stars

Praise for *Beneath White Stars*

"Just when we think that everything has been written about the Holocaust, Holly Mandelkern presents this meditation on the subject that allows readers to feel events in a new way. Holly's poems and lovingly rendered text take readers by the hand and in an intimate way lead us into the personal reality of each individual's life. Taken together, these poems, drawings, and historical sketches show the reader that memory, in the right hands, is a healing art."
> —PHILIP M. SMITH, PhD, Department of History, Texas A&M University

"In a spectrum of soundings, forms, and styles, both fixed and free, we are restored the voices of man, woman, and child, multiplied by millions... In arresting tribute to the lost and to the survivors, Holly Mandelkern's scholarship and her mastery of verse elevate for her readers and for students of the Holocaust, the hardest, and often most poignant, lessons of life, death, and life again."
> —AL ROCHELEAU, author of *On Writing Poetry*

"Having spoken to numerous audiences about the horrors of the Holocaust, I was uplifted by *Beneath White Stars* as it reminds us of the human side of those who suffered. Through this poetry we are able to sense the life and indomitable spirit of the persecuted."
> — HENRY BIRNBREY, survivor and Holocaust educator, Breman Museum, Atlanta, GA

"The poems bring to life a chorus of varied voices portraying in fine, poetic fashion life's lessons in survival, recovery, and redemption. Through captivating illustrations and in the minds and hearts of the reader, these powerfully spiritual voices come to life, remain memorable."
> —STEPHEN CALDWELL WRIGHT, PhD, poet and educator, President and Founder of the Gwendolyn Brooks Writers Association of Florida

"Beneath White Stars is a marvelous, imaginative, and hallowed remembering of the Shoah that illustrates the poet's gift for evoking the unutterable within the rhythms of loss, deprivation, and the reclamation of human dignity. This poetry, enriched by historic narratives and poignant illustrations, echoes themes of Vanderbilt University's Holocaust lecture series, the longest-running lectureship of its kind in American higher education."

> —REVEREND MARK FORRESTER, University Chaplain and Director of Religious Life at Vanderbilt University

"There are rare times when reading a book, particularly one on the Holocaust, one is simply blown away by its content and beauty. Such was the effect on me when I read Holly Mandelkern's *Beneath White Stars*. The combination of magnificent graphics, historical background, and personal reflections in her beautiful poetry makes this a very unusual treatment of the *Shoah*...I look forward to sharing them at Holocaust Memorial services."

> —RABBI FRED GUTTMAN, Mid-Atlantic Regional Director of the International March of the Living and Senior Rabbi of Temple Emanuel in Greensboro, NC

"Holly Mandelkern's poetry goes to the heart of the Holocaust. Historical context and original illustrations accompanying her poems provide a unique and valuable resource for Holocaust students of all ages."

> —HARRIET SEPINWALL, EdD, Professor Emerita, College of Saint Elizabeth Center for Holocaust and Genocide Education, Morristown, NJ

"This remembrance of Holocaust victims and survivors is a stirring and emotional work. The poems inspire deep feeling in the reader, and they are matched by illustrations that give life and nuance to the stories they accompany. Overall, a profoundly moving and thought-provoking work."

> —MARGARET VICKERS, language arts educator, Winter Park, FL

"This rich collection of Holocaust poems by Holly Mandelkern serves a purpose beyond what any analytical treatment of this solemn subject can provide. The poems lend dignity to the suffering, gracing with compelling beauty the sacrifice of so many martyrs of the twentieth century's most horrific catastrophe. The uniqueness and universality of the Holocaust can never be quantified, but the verse presented in this collection does true service to the one purpose to which we must all contribute—remembering. I have been pleased to incorporate some of this fine and emotive poetry into my online course on the history of the Holocaust."

    —KENNETH L. HANSON, PhD, Director of the Judaic Studies Program, University of Central Florida

"In the Holocaust, teachers and students seek meaning from history that defies understanding. With her poetry, Holly Mandelkern brings a unique sensitivity to this quest by restoring dignity to the lives and memories of Holocaust victims. Holly and I have been friends for decades, and I know many of the survivors she has written about with such warmth. The greatest compliment I can give is that my students and I now know them better because of her work."

    —MITCHELL BLOOMER, Holocaust Memorial Resource and Education Center of Florida

Beneath White Stars

Holocaust Profiles in Poetry

Holly Mandelkern

Illustrations by Byron Marshall

AlmondSeed Press

For permission to reproduce selections from this book, please e-mail
HollyMandelkern@gmail.com.

Cover designed by Kilby Creative
Interior layout by Matt Peters at KP Creative
History editor: Mitchell Bloomer
Maps by Mapping Specialists, Ltd.

ISBN: 978-0-9984989-0-4
Library of Congress Control Number: 2016921396
Printed in the United States
E-Book ISBN: 978-0-9984989-2-8

Portions of this work appeared, in both slightly and significantly
different forms, in the following:

Florida State Poets Association Anthology Thirty-Three 2015: "Parallel Limbs"

*Looking Life in the Eye: Poets of Central Florida, Volume Three, A Contemporary
Anthology:* "*L'Chaim*" and "Mr. Sugihara's Eyes"

PRISM: An Interdisciplinary Journal for Holocaust Educators: "Uprooted," as part
of the essay "A Portrait in Poetry: Writing from the Testimony of Roman Kent"
by Holly Mandelkern

Revelry: "Transported"

"Through Leaden Cloud" was a featured poem in the K9s for Warriors
Veterans Day programs in Orlando, Tampa, and Atlantic Beach, Florida, in
November 2014. The poem was set to music by composer Rebekah Todia.

For my father, Herman Lodinger,
of Lead Crew #20, 389th Bombardment Group, July 31, 1944

Through Leaden Cloud

Through leaden cloud we start the flow
of bombs we drop to stop war's blow.
We mark our targets in the sky.
When shot, we parachute—we fly—
some burn—the lucky land and know
we're captive men when asked to show
dog tag and strategy to foe.
We give nothing away. They ply
through leaden cloud.

As we report to camp in tow
to cells, we're prisoners in a row;
on slatted wooden beds we lie.
From ersatz bread, death march friends die
with melt of snow, Allies' hello,
through leaden cloud.

Dr. Janusz Korczak with one of his orphans in the Warsaw Ghetto

Beneath White Stars

*Thank you, Merciful Lord, for having arranged so wisely to provide
flowers with fragrance, glow worms with the glow, and make the stars
in the sky sparkle.*
—DR. JANUSZ KORCZAK,
   Ghetto Diary, Warsaw Ghetto, 1942

*The seed of a creative idea does not die in mud and scum. Even there it
will germinate and spread its blossom like a star shining in darkness.*
—PETR GINZ,
   "Wandering Through Theresienstadt," *Vedem*, Theresienstadt,
   1942–1944

*Under Your white stars
Stretch to me Your white hand.
My words are tears,
Wanting to rest in Your hand . . .*
—AVROM SUTZKEVER,
   "Unter dayne vayse shtern" ("Beneath Your White Stars"), Vilna
   Ghetto, May 22, 1943

Beyond the beds of drifting children,
past the clouded windowpanes,
Doctor praises Grand Designs
of stars surpassing human stains.

Petr tills with intellect
Terezin's mud-engraven ground;
his ideas rise like shining stars
and orbit still, afire, unbound.

From Vilna's silent cellared holes
Avrom beckons God's white hand
to reach beneath His pearly stars—
suspended hope in single strands.

Contents

Elderly man in the Jewish cemetery in Warsaw

Preface

My father, Herman Lodinger, was sent on a death march in Germany in January 1945, but he was not sent from a concentration or death camp. He was a lead bombardier for the US Army Eighth Air Force, and his B-24 had been shot down on July 31, 1944, in the skies over Ludwigshafen, Germany. Two members of his crew were killed in their burning aircraft, and the rest parachuted into enemy territory. He and the surviving crew were interrogated and imprisoned in various prisoner of war camps. My father was sent to Stalag Luft III in Sagan, Germany, one hundred miles southeast of Berlin. He was held at this camp for British and American officers until late January 1945, when the entire prisoner population was marched out into the coldest winter Germany had witnessed in decades.

My father rarely talked about his experience as a lead bombardier or as a prisoner of war. In 1988 Dad sat patiently for hours while I asked questions inspired by a book I had read about Stalag Luft III. He answered readily as if these events had just happened. I could hardly imagine my hardy father reduced to 120 pounds, watching his friends fall asleep in the snow, many never waking up. His account sounded not unlike what Holocaust survivors have described as their own death marches that same winter.

In the summer of 1991 I traveled to Poland and Israel with other teachers to study the Holocaust and Jewish resistance. Starting in Warsaw, our group visited monuments that marked places where Jews had struggled during the Warsaw Ghetto Uprising of 1943. We had our photographs taken with survivors from Warsaw, Vladka and Benjamin Meed, who had brought us there. We walked dirt paths of the historic Jewish cemetery that housed dignified prewar graves and unmarked mass burial sites from the Holocaust years. Suddenly a slight, elderly, bearded man appeared like an apparition and began praying in front of a distinctive gravestone near us. He told me that he was paying respect to his rabbi and that many other rabbis were buried at this

Warsaw cemetery. He asked why we were there: "You will get an idea in your heads about what happened at that time, but you will never know what it was really like. You were not here." Readily I acknowledged that he was right, though we were trying to learn as much as we could. He smiled and touched my shoulder. I knew that his comment would remain with me.

After visiting Auschwitz, Majdanek, and Treblinka in Poland, learning from Holocaust survivors, and studying with scholars and survivors at Yad Vashem and the Ghetto Fighters' House Museum in Israel, I had been exposed to a tremendous amount of valuable information about the Holocaust. These facts and testimonials were the raw material to be used to teach the Holocaust with an emphasis on individual stories. After I returned home and examined my developed film, weeks of taking notes and photographs culminated in weeping. Although the film was processed, I had not finished my own processing of what I had seen and heard at the ghettos, camps, and research centers.

Since that trip, I have continued to study Jewish resistance and have taught this subject at my local teachers' institute for Holocaust studies and at other venues in Central Florida. Over the past few years I have written poems to share this history in a different way. The spare but layered language of poetry seems appropriate for conveying fragments of the lives of those who struggled when pieces are all we can perceive, as the gentleman in Warsaw told me at the start. I see how their lives, dreams, and character opposed the backdrop of death and how their upbringing helped them attempt to stand up for themselves, for a shred of the life they had led before, and often for others. This is true for the Jews of all ages who departed their homes not knowing what was ahead. This is true for those who resisted by writing down their experiences in ghettos and camps, weighing their new circumstances against their past and their hopes for the future. This is true for those who resisted by sustaining others and by arming themselves. This is true for the individuals who rescued others and for those in the aftermath who pursued justice for the criminals and dignity for the innocents.

These then are the themes of the chapters in this book: Departures, Praying in Pencil, Standing in Blood, Rescue, and Roundups. A final chapter, Close Connections, weaves individuals and common threads in the poems together across time and space. It is my hope that *Beneath White Stars* honors the actions and words of those who wrote, spoke, printed, documented, and prayed them.

A Conversation with My Reader

Why did I include history in this book of poetry? Although *Beneath White Stars* is primarily a book of narrative poetry, historical information is critical to appreciate the complex lives of these courageous individuals. The poems give voice to a particular moment, sometimes including the actual voices of the individuals, but the history spans the years of their lives.

Each chapter ends with a section titled "Lost and *Found*," devoted to history about the people and events referenced in the poems. The history thus follows within a few pages' reach of the poems. If you are already well versed in this history, your own background will further inform your reading of the poems. (The purely reflective poems are not accompanied by history.)

Once you have considered the poem and the history, you may find it helpful to revisit the poem. The poem may help you understand or measure the facts by personalizing and infusing these facts with spirit. History and poetry here support each other, lean on each other, and tell about the individuals in different ways.

Through the poetry and history, you will have glimpsed the vitality and ambition of these individuals. The illustrations, too, lend an immediacy to their innocence and to their tenacity and provide yet another way to see the wholeness of their lives. It is this aliveness, even against the backdrop of death, that I hope you will remember. The Hebrew word for remember, *zachor* (pictured next page), marks the end of each "Lost and *Found*" section.

At the back of the book is a timeline that allows you to see how the lives of the people in the poems intersected with one another. The timeline is not a comprehensive chronology of the Holocaust but rather a more personal one for people and events in my poetry. The same personal focus applies to the maps that appear at the end of the "Lost and *Found*" sections.

Departures

Anne Frank

Heartbeats

At Amstelrust Park in Amsterdam Anne Frank
(in photograph dated June '38)
stands beneath trees with sunshine as spotlight,
light summer dress, wide-brimmed hat for shade.

Posed for a shutter, the shining eyes smile—
birthday or outing her parents had planned?
She cradles a dark rabbit close to her body,
feeling its heart beat in her hand.

One palm supports the gentle young creature,
the other hand ready to touch its small face.
Guarded and gauging, the rabbit relaxes
its vigilant ears as it rests in its space.

Immured, though moving in stillness, Anne
with cruel sleight of hand is removed from her ground
where she stands—silent, captive in Amsterdam Annex,
betrayed to the hunters. I hear her heart pound.

Fritz Westfeld in Essen, Germany

The Small World of Little Fritz

For Dr. Fred Westfield

The second floor that houses *Opa*'s toys,
his Essen store, fills Sundays with delight
as miniatures give previews of our lives,
a furtive mix of normal in disguise.

Parades of soldiers, toys that rifle down
to march of beaten drum and thrill of drill,
armed fighters with the proper form of *Heil*
too soon will find their way to my own school.

I roll my engine to the site of fire,
unwind the hose so those inside will live;
I make imagined flames abate unlike
the fire brigades who stand and watch at Night.

I place tin-plated trains around a track,
staid carriages with men on holiday
whose wives and children frolic as they board;
my choo-choo comes, and I'll sit all alone.

Toy soldiers' boots, salutes have schooled our fears;
the blaze of stores and synagogue reroutes
real trains, a children's liberty of sorts,
a one-way trip to newly promised lands.

My notion of America is born
of Indians and cowboys, Mickey Mouse
and Minnie, dancing 'round a metal tin—
a London Bridge for me before their jig.

My hands have tooled a little Torah scroll:
its handles "trees of life" from shopping bags,
a shiny velvet dress for ancient text,
a wooden ark to house the manuscript.
It carves a passage in my boyish heart,
a covenant between uncharted parts.

Opa: colloquial form of Grandpa (German).
Heil: Hail (German).

Watching Myself Watch My Son

I watched myself watch my son
board a train to Britain,
cardboard tag draped around his neck,
his identity number written.

My hands cradled his bowed head;
my mouth asked God to bless him,
keep him close and grant him peace
so far away from Essen.

I left him there as we were told,
instructed not to cry.
I heard myself say I'd soon come;
my lips then said good-bye.

I felt my legs walk me away;
they took me to our home.
The silence of his bedroom meant
the meaning of alone.

The weeks endured, his letter came;
he's well but hoped I'd follow.
Our *Kinder* turned into letters—
my heart felt full yet hollow.

I watched my eyes reread his words,
lips blessed a distant stranger.
Though out of sight I felt the light
that kept him far from danger.

Kinder: children (Yiddish, also German).

Fritz Westfeld on a Kindertransport *train*

Crosscurrents

If England was willing to take all these children, it proved that there was still humanity left somewhere.
—NORBERT WOLLHEIM

Wartime England was flow-charted:
floods of children came, departed,
moved by war and hate.

First wave—the Jewish *Kinder* came
since Nazis set their world aflame,
no sense to sit and wait
for German grip to turn the screw.
They boarded trains,
the lucky few (parents hoped not too late),
with one suitcase,
advice,
good-byes,
trembling knees,
tearful eyes,
a way to change their fate
through Holland's Hook,
Harwich by sea,
to Liverpool Station, London, free
to learn to be a mate.
Ten thousand tales how *Kinder* coped
in homes and hostels
—still they hoped—
"fire-watching" in their new state.

The English simmered fright and ire
of nightly bombs,
London on fire;
the plan, "Pied Piper," porting young
to country gate,

million, near two, far from harm,
spared explosives on a farm
with tears evacuate.

Most English families reunite,
but Jewish children's chances slight—
their parents shipped
like freight.

English people found emotion
for *Kinder* and their own
in motion.
Kindness carried weight.

I Am That Child

I am that child, my suitcase stuffed with clothes,
transported from Berlin, my old hometown.
I am the Jew the Nazi said he loathes;
I rode the rail to live under the Crown.

I am that child transplanted to a home
with Quakers kind who often spoke of Thee.
New London life meant safety and shalom;
each night I doubted I'd see family.

I am that child now called their boy, their lad,
by grown-ups "Uncle Jim" and "Auntie Nell."
In me they looked for good instead of bad;
they taught me right from wrong and fed me well.

I am a man because my parents felt
I could survive where lovingkindness dwelt.

Transported

After the war ended we paraded
to flicker of the film *Bambi*,
even though Sister said we had nothing to celebrate,
the Red Cross letter having just arrived.
In the beginning we rejoiced with furry families
and wobbly-legged little deer prince
who explored under watchful eye of Mother
and wary glance of antlered Father.
We were transported to wooded wonderland,
meadow music and rabbit rhymes.
We watched our story on the large screen:
fires in Frankfurt,
fear of footfalls,
hunt by Man—who was in our city.
"Get up. You must get up."
So we stepped on a train,
fled to English sanctuary,
motherless, with only words
from a pocket dictionary
to help us understand,
"Your mother can't be with you anymore."
We got up,
got out.
Gute Nacht.
We began anew.

Gute Nacht: Good night (German).

Jewish family from Berlin

A Place for Us?

The world seemed to be divided into two parts—those places where the Jews
could not live and those where they could not enter.
—CHAIM WEIZMANN, 1936

We thought there was a face for us
in European nations
but saw our worth was measured out
in *Aktionen* and rations.

We catalogued a case for us,
Vienna's cultured artists,
financiers, and journalists;
Anschluss hit us hardest.

We called Hamburg a place for us,
home for ninety years.
Opa swept up storefront glass
in the Deutschland he revered.

We prayed a ship, a grace for us,
that tripped across the ocean
toward Havana's guarded shores,
waved back without emotion.

Much more than just a phrase for us,
our homeland, Palestine,
was bound in British paper, White,
tied away with twine.

The Polish king's embrace of us
invited us to settle
till Nazis ravaged city Jews
and families of the shtetl.

The Dutch arranged a trace of us
to hide within their house,
silenced us to spare us from
the dreaded knock and *Raus*!

Shaken by this phase for us,
still taken with Paris's charm,
French uniforms broke their word to us,
arrested by gendarmes.

Le Chambon offered praise for us;
Pastor Trocmé modeled how
to love your neighbor as yourself,
five thousand chosen now.

Danes navigated space for us
with boats and friendly hands
that ferried grateful bowed-down heads
to safer Swedish lands.

> *We shall therefore in any given event unequivocally adhere to the concept*
> *that we must obey God before we obey man.*
> —HANS FUGLSANG-DAMGAARD, Lutheran bishop of
> Copenhagen, October 3, 1943

Aktionen: actions (German). Operations carried out against the Jews by
Nazi orders, often for deportation or death.
Anschluss: unification, joining (German). The German incorporation of
Austria in March 1938.
shtetl: a small Jewish village in eastern Europe (Yiddish).
Raus: command meaning "Get out" (German).

Family of Leo Goldberger of Denmark en route to Sweden, October 1943

Packing Her Bag

Frankfurt, October 20, 1941

Forced to leave her Frankfurt home,
she's summoned to the train
with only hours to pack a bag,
no one to explain

how long the trip, the weather there,
belongings she would need;
Mother packed some candlesticks,
fresh-baked bread to feed . . .

Yes, she said to ballet shoes,
doubted *pas de deux*,
but left behind her warmest boots,
without the proper clues,

tossed her frayed and favorite dress,
no room in her small bags;
"relocating to the east,"
she'd soon be wearing rags.

She held her piano music sheets,
nocturnes, Beethoven, Brahms,
picked her slimmest book of prayers,
not leaving without Psalms,

Rainer Maria Rilke's poems,
Goethe for the rail,
not knowing all she'd really need
were water and a pail.

Wrapped in woolen winter skirt
to cover her bare knees,
she wore her coat, a warm-up suit
for dying by degrees.

She buried asthma medicine,
the scant supply prescribed;
she'd learn to breathe a lethal air
with treatment improvised.

In truth she'd need a dose of luck,
skills to measure food,
a sleuth to get her slice of bread,
a star that named her *Jude*.

She pressed her life into a satchel
filled with precious stuff,
but to survive in Ghetto Łódź,
things were not enough.

Jude: Jew (German).

Watching My Daughter Pack Her Bag

Frankfurt, October 20, 1941

Forced to leave Frankfurt tonight,
she looks to me with forlorn gaze—
what should she take?
We must pack light.
Will we be gone for months, days?
There's little time and loaves to bake.

She grasps her locket, charms, ring,
ballet slippers, Beethoven, Brahms,
Goethe for the train,
velvet jewelry box that sings,
childhood diary, Rilke, Psalms,
slicker if it rains,

winter coat, prescription pills,
sturdy shoes, snapshots of Brother.
A last look back, she turns to stare;
her wide eyes fill.
I, her mother,
can only brush her hair.

Father Patrick Desbois in Ukraine

Lost and *Found*

When excavating sites in the villages in Ukraine where mobile killing squads murdered Jews, the French Catholic priest Father Patrick Desbois and his team of linguists, historians, ballistic experts, and photographers often uncover Stars of David pendants and wedding bands on the ground. Just moments before their deaths, Jewish women cast these stars and rings to the ground so that their killers would not derive benefit from them. For most of the women, this action was their last and perhaps their only moment of defiance. Upon discovery of the tarnished jewelry, Father Desbois describes the moment: "Finally we found you."

The pages that follow convey some of what we know of what was lost and what has been found, studied, analyzed, photographed, mapped, and documented about the individuals and events you just encountered in the poems in this chapter. This format is followed in all the chapters except the last.

Heartbeats

A photograph of a girl holding a rabbit in a park, dated June 1938, provides a snapshot of daily life for a Jewish family in Amsterdam before war and its harsh measures came to their city. This girl is Anne Frank (1929–1945), probably the most well-known young diarist from the Holocaust years.

After Hitler rose to power in 1933, Otto Frank moved his business and family from Frankfurt, Germany, where the Frank family had lived since the seventeenth century, to Amsterdam to provide a safer place for them to live. Here he started a business selling pectin, a powdered fruit extract used to make jam, and in 1938 a second company selling herbs to season meat. Here Anne biked to school and played with friends and neighbors. She enjoyed going to parties and to her neighborhood ice cream parlor. She was interested in history and Greek mythology, writing, boys, and cats and dogs.

Otto Frank took dozens of photographs of his beloved daughters, Anne and Margot. He probably took this one of Anne cradling a rabbit at Amstelrust Park by the Amstel River, not far from their Amsterdam home. Perhaps she was celebrating her ninth birthday, June 12, 1938, on this outing.

The German invasion of the Netherlands began on May 10, 1940. By mid-May, the country was under German occupation. The Frank family went into hiding on July 6, 1942, and lived in shadow for more than two years. They were discovered and arrested by the Gestapo on August 4, 1944.

The Small World of Little Fritz
Watching Myself Watch My Son
Crosscurrents
I Am That Child
Transported

The *Kindertransport* attempted to save Jewish children predominantly from Germany, Austria, Czechoslovakia, and even some sites in Poland. The danger of living in these lands became palpable amidst burned synagogues, arrests, murders, and the destruction of Jewish-owned stores throughout Germany and Austria from November 9 to November 10, 1938, the time that became known as *Kristallnacht*, the Night of Broken Glass. British public opinion and relentless efforts by refugee aid committees convinced British authorities to allow these children from ages five to nearly seventeen to enter the United Kingdom without their parents. Private individuals or organizations agreed to pay their expenses.

From December 1938 through the beginning of September 1939 Jewish parents voluntarily sent approximately ten thousand children to the relative safety of Great Britain, first by train, then by ship across the Channel. Escorts accompanied the children, and parents were given instructions about saying good-bye. Norbert Wollheim, a twenty-five-year-old Jew from Berlin who helped administer the *Kindertransport* operation and who is quoted in the epigraph for "Crosscurrents," served as one of these escorts. For the younger children this was often their first time away from their families. Some of the older teens viewed the journey as something of an adventure.

Where would the *Kinder* find shelter? The children were dispersed to private homes or to group settings such as hostels, boardinghouses, and farms in England, Scotland, Wales, and Northern Ireland. Individuals and families of different faiths, including Jews and Christians of many denominations, notably Quakers, housed the refugees. In particular, the Quakers helped convince the British government to relax immigration rules, and they escorted children to the trains and greeted them when they arrived in Great Britain. Thousands of Quakers kept Jewish children in their homes.

When war seemed imminent, there was concern for the safety of all children in Britain. Many British parents sent their children to the countryside for safety, some privately but most under the auspices of the government's Operation Pied Piper. Nearly two million British schoolchildren, usually accompanied by their teachers, were sent away in the first few days of September 1939 in response to the order of August 31 to "evacuate forthwith." The Jewish *Kinder* were included in these resettlements. The expected bombings did not begin when predicted, however, and within a few months more than half of the children were returned to their homes in the cities. When Germans actually started nightly bombings of English cities in September 1940, all children in urban settings, including the *Kinder* who had returned to London and to other large cities, were vulnerable.

Most of the *Kinder* learned to speak English, and all tried to adjust to a different culture. Children missed their families and were allowed to write to their parents; parents longed for their children, who became "children turned into letters" (Kaplan), an adaptation of the German phrase "children grow up to be people." Most of these children never saw their parents again and sometimes received news of the death of their parents in a letter from the Red Cross. Some never heard anything at all. While many British schoolchildren celebrated the end of the war by going to see the film *Bambi*, some of the Jewish children had little to celebrate and recognized Bambi's plight as their own ("Kindertransport," *The Reunion*).

The experience of Fritz Westfeld (b. 1926), later known as Fred Westfield, is one of ten thousand stories of the *Kindertransport*. The situation of the Jews was worsening in Germany, and Fritz's parents felt that leaving the country was the best response. Fritz's father was an attorney in Essen, Germany, and Fritz's maternal grandparents ran a store selling housewares and toys. After *Kristallnacht* swept through their hometown, his parents decided that Fritz should seek shelter in England. His father had already taken his older brother, Erich, to live with an uncle in Nashville, Tennessee, in 1936. (The uncle had settled there because his wife was a native of Nashville.) Another uncle, Walter Westfeld, an eminent art dealer in nearby Düsseldorf, was accused of smuggling art and foreign exchange violations and was arrested two weeks after *Kristallnacht*. This uncle was tried and imprisoned, and his art was auctioned off. Funds from Uncle Walter's business were available to the family to help with resettlement efforts, but the family was cautious about using these resources. (Walter Westfeld would later be killed at Auschwitz.)

In January 1939 twelve-year-old Fritz boarded the train for England alone, waving good-bye to his parents, aware of the strong chance that they might not reunite. He was taken through the Netherlands to Harwich, England, and then to the Jewish immigrant family in London who would shelter him. "Every night I doubted whether I would ever see my parents again," he later explained (Robbins). He knew little English but had studied a few phrases in preparation for the move. When the war began in September 1939, Fritz was moved again, along with thousands of other children, to the countryside. He was placed in the home of a non-Jewish family with whom he bonded quite well.

Dr. Fred Westfield

Because his parents expected to gain entry into the United States in a short time, they were allowed to reside temporarily in London in the summer of 1939, as were other German Jewish families. In the summer of 1940, along with other German Jewish men, his father was placed in an internment camp because of suspicions that he might be a German spy. Fritz rejoined his mother in London, and in the fall of 1940 he and his parents left by ship for New York through waters infested with German submarines, soon settling in Nashville to be reunited with his brother, Erich, and his aunt and uncle. Here Fritz became Fred and his last name was adapted to the less German-sounding

Westfield. Another uncle, Max Westfield, a portrait painter, also came to Nashville at this time.

In Nashville Fred started public school, and when he was almost sixteen, he participated in a work-study program to learn the trade of watchmaking to help support the family. His father, a recipient of the Iron Cross as a judge advocate during World War I, worked in bookkeeping, not permitted to practice law since he was licensed only in a foreign country. After graduation from high school Fred worked in the jewelry business, and in 1945 he joined the US Army as an instructor, applying his watchmaking skills to repairing optical instruments.

With help from the GI Bill, Fred Westfield entered Vanderbilt University in 1947, as had his brother, Erich. Here he earned his economics degree in three years and graduated magna cum laude. He earned his PhD at Massachusetts Institute of Technology, taught at Northwestern University, and became a professor of economics at Vanderbilt University, on the faculty from 1965 to 1998. He has since served as Professor of Economics Emeritus.

A Place for Us?

The danger that started in Germany and Austria did not end there. Yet the search for safer places to live began only when Jews across Europe were certain of the urgency of their situation. Jews had lived in Germany, Austria, Poland, the Netherlands, and France for hundreds of years and had created productive lives there, both personally and communally. When finally convinced of the need to leave, they had to find places to go.

Although there were warning signs when Adolf Hitler became chancellor, German Jews were reluctant to leave their homes, businesses, professions, and beloved homeland. Patriotic feelings were the norm for German Jews. One hundred thousand had volunteered to fight for Germany during World War I, and twelve thousand had died in combat. Thousands had been decorated and had served as officers in the field. But by 1936 the viability of Jewish communal life was uncertain in Germany, as noted after the war by Israel's first president, Chaim Weizmann. From 1933 through 1938 approximately one-third of Germany's Jews emigrated because of worsening conditions.

When Germany annexed Austria in March 1938, the Austrian Jews—including bankers, journalists, actors, writers, doctors, lawyers, artists, and art collectors—immediately became targets of Nazi abuse, as they had been in Germany. *Kristallnacht* heightened the dilemma of how German and Austrian Jews could depart. The process of emigration, already complicated, now worsened with the "Aryanization" of Jewish businesses, leaving once financially secure individuals nearly destitute, thereby making it harder for them to relocate.

Jewish chaplain in the German army, World War I

Shtetl life in Poland,
after the photographs of Roman Vishniac

Where could a Jew go? At the Évian Conference of July 1938, representatives of thirty-two countries discussed allowing additional Jews to enter their lands after seeing the endangered status of Jews in Germany. Only the Dominican Republic offered to accept more Jews, raising the nation's limit to one hundred thousand, and Denmark and the Netherlands offered temporary asylum. These offers of sanctuary were not enough to shelter the masses in need of new homes.

Similarly, the British controlled the territory of Palestine (the land that later would become Israel) and issued a White Paper on May 17, 1939, that limited the number of Jewish immigrants into Palestine to seventy-five thousand from 1939 through 1944. On May 13, 1939, the SS *St. Louis* carried about 930 Jews who sought shelter across the Atlantic Ocean, but they were not accepted at the prearranged destination of Cuba. Almost all were sent back to Europe, and Belgium, the Netherlands, France, and Great Britain took them in. More than half of those returned to Europe were in danger again when the German army occupied Belgium, the Netherlands, and France. Those who had disembarked in Great Britain were safe.

A Jewish presence had existed in Poland since the fourteenth century, when the Jews were invited by King Casimir III to settle there. When Poland fell in September 1939, harsh regulations and abusive treatment began for the more than two million Jews living under German occupation. When the German forces invaded the Soviet Union and Soviet-occupied eastern Poland in June 1941, more than one million additional Jews fell under their control and were killed outright.

Wherever the Germans assailed, Jews became targets of Nazi oppression. Regulations against the Jews of Germany that had taken years to implement took only days to affect the Jews of the newly occupied western European countries. Otto Frank, Anne's father, was among those who had departed from Germany in search of a more secure life but who were caught in the Nazi web again when the Germans invaded the Netherlands on May 10, 1940. Many Dutch individuals participated in hiding Jews, yet these generous offers did not always succeed in saving lives.

The German invasion of France in May 1940 left Jews vulnerable not only to the Nazis but also to more than four thousand compliant French police who rounded up 13,152 Jews, mainly foreign-born, in Paris on July 16, 1942. The Nazi hunter Serge Klarsfeld stated that 80 percent of these arrests were made by French uniforms. In contrast, Le Chambon-sur-Lignon, France, a village with many Huguenot Protestants whose ancestors had suffered as a minority religion, offered refuge to the Jews who traveled to their village. Pastor André Trocmé, his wife, and their nephew set examples of compassion by sheltering all Jews, especially children, who made their way to Le Chambon. Their parishioners willingly followed their example, thus saving about five thousand lives from December 1940 to September 1944.

On October 1–2, 1943, the Danish resistance ferried 7,200 Danish Jews to safety in Sweden, thus saving most of the country's Jews. The family of Dr. Leo Goldberger was among them.

A family in the shtetl, Poland

Packing Her Bag
Watching My Daughter Pack Her Bag

After the Nazis came to power, the Jews who stayed in Germany experienced a dramatic reduction of their quality of life. The forced departure of the Jews of Frankfurt, Germany, to the ghettos of Poland is one measure of this descent.

The Jewish community in Frankfurt was one of the largest and most important in Europe. A cultural center of the Haskalah (Enlightenment) and the home of the eminent philosophers Franz Rosenzweig and Martin Buber, Frankfurt was also a hub of commerce, industry, and banking. In 1930 the Jewish community numbered thirty thousand, and Frankfurt had a Jewish mayor.

The Jews regarded themselves as proud citizens of Germany and were entrenched in the rich cultural life Germany offered them. Many accounts relate the love of German Jews, including teens in the upper grades, for the works of the German writers Goethe, Schiller, and Rilke and the music of the German composers. In 1933, when Jewish artists were expelled from their positions with German orchestras, opera companies, and theater groups, they formed their own cultural organizations. Frankfurt had one such magnificent *Kulturbund* orchestra. However, the Nazis would not permit Jewish cultural organizations to perform the music of most German composers, such as Beethoven and Mozart.

In 1933, with Hitler in power, physical and economic attacks on the Jewish community began. Amidst antisemitic propaganda and financial regulations (more than 530 Jewish-owned businesses closed that year), many Jews left Frankfurt, including Otto Frank and his family. By May 1939, even before the start of war, more than half of the Jews had fled.

Responding to hardships, the extant Jewish community set up a network of welfare organizations, but conditions worsened in Frankfurt. By February 1940 many were forced to leave their apartments and move in with others, turning their apartments over to German authorities. Forced labor began for some in March 1941, and deportation out of the country to ghettos in Łódź, Minsk, and Kovno followed in the fall. By September 1941 fewer than eleven thousand Jews remained in Frankfurt. In 1942 Frankfurt's Jews were sent to the death camps of Majdanek and Sobibór in German-occupied Poland and to Theresienstadt (also known as Terezin), near Prague. Most sent after that time were deported to Theresienstadt.

The transport mentioned in the poem left Frankfurt on October 20, 1941, and arrived in the Łódź Ghetto two days later. (Some accounts say that the train left on October 21.) The Jews were given very little time to pack and had strict regulations on baggage they could carry. They, along with most of the other Jews in German-occupied Europe, were not told of their true destinations. For most on this transport, the Łódź Ghetto was not the last stop on their deadly journey.

NORWAY
SWEDEN
Scotland
NORTH SEA
Northern Ireland
UNITED KINGDOM
IRELAND
DENMARK
Copenhagen
Hamburg
Wales
England
Harwich
London
Amsterdam
NETHERLANDS
Berlin
Essen
Düsseldorf
ENGLISH CHANNEL
BELGIUM
GERMANY
Terezin/ Theresienstadt
Prague
Frankfurt
CZECH REPUBLIC
Paris
Vienna
FRANCE
AUSTRIA
SWITZERLAND
Évian
SLOVENIA
Le Chambon-sur-Lignon
CROATIA
ADRIATIC SEA
ITALY
SPAIN
MEDITERRANEAN SEA

Praying in Pencil

Gertrud Kolmar of Berlin

Between the Lines

Women wrote in darkest times
when Nazis censored speech and rhymes,
banished thoughts and youthful dreams,
metered minds, measured schemes.

Jewish women left us traces,
fragments of their narrow spaces,
placed their words inside the staves
that contradicted narrow graves.

Some shaped lines as simple ballad,
penciled hopes, their bodies pallid.
Pen on paper gave life meaning,
snapshots of what souls were gleaning.

They dreamed of living through their fears;
their poems framed the nightmare years.
They told the truth of ghetto lives,
of camps where husbands lost their wives,

of Holy Writ and ridicule,
abandonment of Golden Rule,
purges, dirges, sad refrains,
sanctity amidst the stains.

Gertrud Kolmar, poet of faces,
paraphrased the "ruined gazes,"
Dachau's murders cut and branded,
bodies out of souls slip, stranded.

Miriam Ulinover, Ghetto Łódź,
the Yiddish poet, gentle judge,
versed herself with evidence
that tradition was a sturdy fence.

Her shtetl girls in weekday dress
wore good sides out for *Shabes* best,
but ghettos fashioned heavy skirts,
worn with worry and alert.

Chava Rosenfarb, the youngest guest
at Miriam's table, composed a test:
Isaac, risen from Bible days,
entreated her to meet his gaze,

walk beside him toward the altar,
love afire, no time to falter.
She countered Isaac's binding plea;
her fate was forged, but he could flee.

In camps the Karmel sisters wrote
their rhyme-and-rhythm's antidote;
their seamless poems measured stresses
sewn into the hems of dresses.

Henia (camp name: nine zero six)
wrote, recited verses fixed:
"cemetery days," "fog and gloom,"
mental haven from this doom.

Ilona's couplets screamed the truth
of cursed dreams and ruined youth:
"your pen, your shovel," "ink of tears,"
transplanted words that disappear.

From Sweden's shelter, Nelly Sachs
named the stokers of smokestacks—
"O the Chimneys"—killing dear
to mind of master "puppeteer."

Her words uncloaked the cost of error—
shadows, stones, and stars felt terror,
children wept, their mothers shattered,
choral pleas of those who mattered.

The "long rehearsal" for one's death
made still life and labored breath—
gentle when you teach us now
to live again, from hell, and how.

Sisters Henia and Ilona Karmel,
after a photo taken in the garden of the Karolinska Institute,
Stockholm, 1946

Alma Rosé

In Auschwitz Alma Rosé led
an orchestra of lives that fed
the virtuosa heart
whose only respite was its art.

Chopin's études summoned songs
of life remembered, present wrongs,
crescendo of the concert hall,
morendo of their tragic fall.

Hannah Senesh's sands, seas,
lightning flashes set her free
to lift from Zion up so high
like sacred fire in the sky.

The parachute was her dispatch
and she the burning "blessed match"
who tried to warn Hungarian Jews;
she gave her life to bring them news.

Gerty Spies from Terezin penned,
wondered how survivors mend
with beating heart a "silent stone,"
children searching for their home.

Trude Groag, Terezin nurse,
honored patients in her verse.
Terezin women—teachers, writers,
poets, artists, freedom fighters—

ghetto women told their stories,
echoed simple girlhood glories,
memories in metaphor
enjambing better years before.

In the camps like pencils broken
women graphed a life unspoken,
encrypting nouns, inventing verbs,
describing with imperfect words.

Others, too, wrote poetry;
in their thoughts they could be free.
They measured words; they used their minds.
They wrote and read between the lines.

shtetl: a small Jewish village in eastern Europe (Yiddish).
Shabes: Sabbath (Yiddish).

Hannah Senesh in Palestine before her parachute mission

Anne's view of the horse chestnut tree from the Annex

Parallel Limbs

Pavel Friedmann and Anne Frank
drew comfort from a tree,
a private avenue, aligned—
alone, majestic, free.

Anne's horse chestnut dressed the yard
in shades of leafy green;
painted birds in bluest skies
traced what life had been.

Enfolding arms of open air,
envisioned, stilled her fear,
solace for the suffering,
dewdrop for the tear.

No ghetto hosted butterflies,
but Pavel praised the bright
yellow-fingered dandelions,
climbing branches, white

chestnut shoulders, boyhood spells,
aloft where sentries played,
grateful for familiar things,
fortresses of shade.

Amsterdam, Theresienstadt:
two loved the sturdy limbs.
In simple words they lauded them
and penned their private hymns.

Dandelions in Terezin

You Never Saw Another Butterfly

You tell us of the butterfly
whose yellow dazzled you,
kissed the ghetto world good-bye—
the last bright winged one flew.

The sun's tears like your own fears
"sing against a white stone . . ."*
The sun can cry, but you must dry
your tears inside a poem.

For seven weeks you gaze about
for signs of what's still living:
dandelions, white chestnut branch,
your reasons for thanksgiving.

You miss the flight of butterflies—
"O happy living things."†
We mourn your own departure there,
a poet without wings.

*Pavel Friedmann, "The Butterfly."
†Samuel Taylor Coleridge, "The Rime of the Ancient Mariner."

Petr Ginz in Prague,
after a painting by Petr Ginz

Overdue: Book Reports, May–September 1944

The library clerk, no longer surprised,
smiled when Petr brought
volumes to the Central Library:
Descartes's *Discourse on Method,*
sociology texts,
pedagogies,
Wells's *A Short History of the World,*
Letters of Seneca, the Stoic.

Books led him past the brick
to ancient times,
stars and skies,
Jack London's frozen lands,
Moonlit Mountain,
home, to Prague.

The patron, scribe himself,
balanced Balzac's Parisian passions
and Gorky's Russian woes
with detective novels
and astronomical abstracts.

In September, Petr picked
A Christmas Carol (miser repents),
Rembrandt (fellow artist of the dark),
Oscar Wilde's *De Profundis* (sin and forgiveness),
Thomas Mann's *Mario and the Magician* (Fascists fall),
Albert Schweitzer's life and thoughts.

All that October
the library clerk
did not smile;

Petr Ginz,
the sixteen-year-old patron,
did not return
to the Ghetto Central Library,
Terezin.

Ka-du the Monster,
after Jules Verne and Petr Ginz

Lines in Space

Well, I feel that we should always put a little art into what we do. It's better that way.
    —JULES VERNE, *From the Earth to the Moon*

Young da Vinci.

Petr Ginz, number 446,
leaving Prague on a forced trip,
22/October/42, night,
on an unnamed transport
to Theresienstadt,
packed his bags,
kept a mental log
of his ten-kilogram limit (rather light):
tools to illustrate his book
on wizards and mountains (a manuscript),
paper, endpaper, thin leather to bind,
his Jules Verne favorites
left behind.
He took a few broken watercolor paints,
linocut knives for rockets, ships.
With woodcuts he saw the same
arches,
planes,
curves,
calm lines.
His precious suitcase
he hoped to find.

Petr Ginz, 1880 his number,
forced on a trip
to unfamiliar parts,
28/September/44,

no provisions for food
or slumber,
calmly left Theresienstadt.
He knew this world
through how they swore
but drew world maps,
Moon Landscape,
charts.
Linocut knives
had schooled his heart.
He traveled far through Jules Verne's art,
his own journeys now cut short,
a private universe
left behind.

Waiting for him to board the train,
sister reached to touch his hand
that now held two pieces of bread,
nothing for his piercing mind.

—————————

Petrginz,
asteroid 50413,
named by two astronomers (Czech),
orbits the sun every four-plus years—
(golden asteroids, Verne's frontiers)
arches,
arcsecs,
apogees,
planes,
calm lines,
curves,
degrees,

lines in space—
Petr's spheres.

Petr Ginz on the moon

Dr. Emanuel Ringelblum in the Warsaw Ghetto

So the World Would Know

Any superfluous word, any literary exaggeration grated and repelled. Jewish life during the war is so packed with events that it is unnecessary to add an extra sentence . . .

—EMANUEL RINGELBLUM, "Essay on Oyneg Shabbes" in *Notes from the Warsaw Ghetto (Ksovim fun Geto)*

He wrote their lives so all would know these Jews—
their shtetls, stories, songs, and golden dreams—
in archives so that we could see the hues.

Of ghetto life in Warsaw we have clues,
collected by these young and academes.
He wrote their lives so all would know these Jews.

His *Oyneg Shabes* group recorded news,
filed crimson-coded papers by the reams
in archives so that we could see the hues.

The sea of yellow stars unveiled abuse;
the voices of resistance showed brave schemes.
He wrote their lives so all would know these Jews.

To stay or run away he had to choose;
he stayed to write their fight against extremes
in archives so that we could see the hues.

When ghetto fighters pieced together cues,
they buried evidence beneath the beams.
He wrote their lives so all would know these Jews
in archives so that we could see the hues.

Oyneg Shabes: Joy of the Sabbath (Yiddish).

Milk can holding documents collected by the Oyneg Shabes

Lost and *Found*

The poet Trude Groag teaching art at Terezin

Between the Lines

Unbelievably, many women (and men) wrote poetry during these terrible times. Some of the women poets are cited in this poem. Why did they write? Some preserved the prewar past as a way of holding on to precious memories, while others wrote to document current events and to keep their spirits alive in these terrible times.

Henia and Ilona Karmel tell us in the 1947 preface to their poems that they wrote so their experiences would serve as a warning for future generations, a cry to "Remember!"

Gertrud Kolmar (1894–1943), a lyric poet from Berlin, reflected on the impact of the camps such as Dachau in her poem "In the Camp" (1933). She was taken to a forced labor camp and then murdered soon after her arrival in Auschwitz. She left behind hundreds of poems and many poignant letters, most of which are known because she sent them to relatives outside of Germany.

Miriam Ulinover (1890–1944), a prolific and well-known Yiddish poet from Łódź, wrote of traditional Jewish life. She held a writers' circle at her home in the Łódź Ghetto from 1940 through the spring of 1944 and nurtured other writers, although meeting was a forbidden activity. She was taken to Auschwitz in August 1944 and was murdered there. Some of her beloved poems were placed into the Oyneg Shabes Archive in Warsaw and then recovered after the war. Perhaps one of the many Łódź refugees who worked in the archive had carried her poems into the Warsaw Ghetto.

Chava Rosenfarb (1923–2011), also from Łódź, became at age seventeen the youngest poet to join the writers' group at Miriam Ulinover's home at the invitation of the great ghetto poet Simcha-Bunim Shayevitch. After hiding for a short time, she and her family were sent to Auschwitz, where her poems were cast into a pile to be discarded. From this camp, she, her sister, and her mother were sent to a camp near Hamburg to build houses for Germans. Here she wrote some of her poems in tiny letters on the ceiling above her bed and memorized them. She and her sister and mother were then taken to Bergen-Belsen, where she was suffering from typhus when the camp was liberated on April 15, 1945. Later that year the three Rosenfarb women crossed into Belgium, and Chava lived as a displaced person. She married in 1949 and moved to Canada, where she continued to write poetry and later fiction. She has been hailed as a major Yiddish writer.

Sisters Henia (1923–1984) and Ilona (1925–2000) Karmel wrote and recited poems in several camps where they were imprisoned. Most of their poems were written after working twelve-hour shifts at Skarżysko-Kamienna in central Poland. The poems were written in pencil on the blank sides of work sheets given to them by a non-Jewish worker in the plant. When they were sent to a forced labor camp attached to Buchenwald, the sisters protected their poems by sewing them inside the hems of their dresses. The sisters and their mother were marched from Buchenwald in April 1945; all were seriously injured, and their mother died. Fearing death, Henia saw a cousin and tore poems from her dress, entrusting them with the cousin and asking her to give them to Henia's husband. The poems survived, as did Henia and Ilona, and were published in 1947. Henia later sent one of her poems, "Christ Lonely," to Pope John Paul II, a childhood friend of her husband from Kraków. Ilona later served as a lecturer at MIT in creative writing from 1979 to 1995. Henia continued to write as well.

Trude Groag nursing at Terezin

In 1940 Nelly Sachs (1891–1970) fled from her birthplace, Berlin, to Sweden, where she wrote about the plight of her fellow Jews. She received the Nobel Prize in Literature in 1966.

In Auschwitz Alma Rosé (1906–1944) conducted the women's orchestra and wrote lyrics and at least one poem. A former concert violinist (and niece of composer-conductor Gustav Mahler), she motivated the women to play their best at Auschwitz-Birkenau to stay alive, and many of their lives were spared because she refined their musical talent. At its height, the orchestra numbered forty-five to fifty women. She herself died from illness at this death camp.

Originally from Budapest before moving to Palestine as a teen, Hannah Senesh (1921–1944) returned to Europe as a member of the British military forces in March 1944. Her task was to parachute into Yugoslavia and proceed to her native Hungary to help Allied pilots shot down behind Nazi lines and to aid Jews of Hungary. She was one of thirty-two parachutists from Palestine on this mission. While Hannah Senesh was with the Yugoslavian partisans, she wrote the poem "Blessed Is the Match" in May 1944, showing that she fully knew the perils of her work.

From Yugoslavia Hannah Senesh crossed into Hungary to make contact with the Jewish community. She was captured, tried in a Hungarian court, and executed as a traitor to Hungary by the empowered Fascist party, Arrow Cross, in November 1944. She left a final note for her comrades: "Continue on the way, don't be deterred. Continue the struggle till the end, until the day of liberty comes, the day of victory for our people." Her courage and her poems are still revered, especially in Israel.

From Theresienstadt (Terezin), a camp that imprisoned many artists, Trude Groag (1890–1979) of Moravia in Czechoslovakia wrote about her patients while serving as both nurse and preschool art teacher. An adult daughter of Theodor Herzl, the late nineteenth-century founder of political Zionism and architect of the Jewish state, was one of her patients. At this same camp Gerty Spies (1897–1997) used vivid imagery to show the challenges of surviving. A German Jew, she first began writing poetry in Terezin.

Parallel Limbs
You Never Saw Another Butterfly

Anne Frank (1929–1945) received from her parents a hardbound diary with a red-and-white-checkered pattern on her thirteenth birthday (June 12, 1942), and she began recording impressions two days later. Within a month, her family was in hiding. While the world outside was forbidden to her, Anne kept writing about what she could see through the attic window. In February, April, and May 1944 she described with joy the horse chestnut tree in the courtyard below.

When her father, Otto Frank, read her diary after the war, he was surprised by the delight the tree had provided. Although this horse chestnut tree fell down in August 2010, many people and institutions around the world had already planted its sapling descendants.

Pavel Friedmann (1921–1944) was born in Prague and was deported to Theresienstadt (Terezin) on April 26, 1942. In this camp he wrote the poem "The Butterfly" with its famous line "Only I never saw another butterfly." Although imprisoned, he found what he loved there: "The dandelions call to me / And the white chestnut branches in the court." The poem is dated June 4, 1942, and is preserved in its typewritten form on thin paper as part of a collection in the Jewish Museum in Prague. Pavel died in Auschwitz on September 29, 1944.

Overdue: Book Reports, May-September 1944
Lines in Space

Petr Ginz (1928–1944) of Prague was a child prodigy—an artist, avid reader, aficionado of Jules Verne, and prolific writer of poetry, essays, and novels. When the German army entered Czechoslovakia and occupied Prague on March 15, 1939, life as usual changed for Petr. As a child of a Jewish father and a non-Jewish mother, he was classified by the Germans as a *Mischling* (part Jew, mixed breed) of the first degree, as was his sister, Eva (Chava). Within four months of the occupation, legislation was implemented against Jews and *Mischlinge*, restricting their activities. By September 1941 Jews were required to wear a yellow Star of David. Deportations to the concentration camp of Theresienstadt in the city of Terezin began during December 1941, and Petr was taken on a transport in October 1942 when he was fourteen and a half. His sister was taken to Terezin in May 1944.

While living in Prague, Petr kept a diary with terse, mature responses to living under the German shadow. He kept records of his academic, literary, and artistic goals and accomplishments, setting very high standards for himself. Beginning in October 1943, he kept a journal as a prisoner in Terezin with monthly "Plans" for his proposed accomplishments and "Reports" of his actual achievements. The Plans and Reports show an extremely ambitious and urgent effort to study, read, create, write, and draw in the face of death. By fifteen he was extremely well-read and politically astute, and he had already written several novels, poetry, and an Esperanto-Czech dictionary before he was sent from his home. *A View from Prehistory* is his only surviving book. Professing that Jules Verne authored the manuscript, Petr actually wrote and illustrated the tale of Ka-du, a Mesozoic monster that resembled a dinosaur but was in reality a robot that terrorized natives of the Belgian Congo. His skills as a visual artist were equally impressive, and he continued his woodcuts, linocuts, and drawings at Terezin, including *Moon Landscape*. Using the library at Terezin, he read voraciously. The range of his interests, as reflected in his art and writing, was immense and imaginative.

He wrote some of his most masterful pieces as the editor of *Vedem* (Czech for "We Lead" or "In the Lead"). This collective and secret publication featured prose, poetry, essays, jokes, literary reviews, news, and drawings by the approximately one hundred boys, ages thirteen though fifteen, of Home One, a room in Terezin's Building L-417. "Linocuts" from 1943, about the role of emotion and discipline in creating art, showcases his maturity and gift of expression. The line "You can know the world through its curses" appears in his "The Life of an Inanimate Object." In December 1942, just months after his arrival at Terezin, *Vedem* began appearing weekly, with Petr writing articles, editing, and completing the volume if others had not written enough.

Petr was deported to Auschwitz on September 28, 1944, and died there. The volumes of *Vedem* were recovered after the war's end by one of the boy survivors from the barrack, Sidney Taussig, who had buried them in a metal container beneath the blacksmith shop where his father worked. The eight hundred pages of *Vedem* are housed at the Terezin Memorial in the Czech Republic.

Petr's art, a collection of two hundred pieces, including *Moon Landscape*, was donated to Yad Vashem by his father. When Israeli astronaut Ilan Ramon consulted Yad Vashem about taking a meaningful remembrance of the Holocaust on his space voyage in 2003, the museum recommended a copy of Petr Ginz's *Moon Landscape*. After the tragic disintegration of the space shuttle *Columbia* and the publicity given to Petr's drawing, a query came to Yad Vashem from a man from Prague who remembered seeing artwork of a similar style in the attic of the home he had purchased. He wondered if the same person might have done the drawing. The home was the residence of close friends of the Ginz family, and Petr's sister, Chava, verified that the artwork and journal in the attic were Petr's. The diary has since been edited by his sister and published.

Petr was devoted to science, science fiction, space fantasy, and adventure. In 2000 two Czech astronomers discovered an asteroid and named it Petrginz in honor of this gifted young man.

So the World Would Know

Dr. Emanuel Ringelblum (1900–1944) was uniquely qualified to establish and oversee the biggest underground archival collection, the Oyneg Shabes (also spelled Oyneg Shabbes or Oneg Shabbat) Archive, in occupied Europe. Before the war he headed YIVO, an organization founded in Vilna to encourage scholarship in Yiddish. He had organized laypeople and professional historians to gather historical information, including folklore, jokes, music, and songs of the Jews of Poland. By 1939 as a historian he had already published 126 scholarly articles.

Dr. Ringelblum also had experience in Jewish communal work through the Joint Distribution Committee, a Jewish self-help organization. In the fall of 1938 he assisted Jews of Polish citizenship who had been expelled from Germany and were stranded in Zbąszyń, Poland. He organized community kitchens, Yiddish lessons, and Yiddish theater to give them support and hope. (Only so much could be done, though: a despairing letter from emigrant Jews in Zbąszyń to their son in Paris so radicalized the boy that he shot and killed a German diplomat—the excuse the Nazis had been waiting for to set in motion the violence of *Kristallnacht*.) Later he coordinated the Joint's establishment of loan societies and self-help house committees to deal with deprivation during the Nazi occupation of Poland.

Early on, Dr. Ringelblum recognized that life under the Germans in the Warsaw Ghetto was unprecedented and therefore worthy of thorough documentation. For this end he organized a cadre of professional historians and amateur assistants to collect the data, and the organization officially came together in November 1940 as Oyneg Shabes. The group often met on Sabbath afternoons and took its name from this meeting time. The members assembled documents from the Germans, the underground, political parties, and cultural organizations, as well as private letters, postcards, diaries, and works of art. Desiring information to be gathered as events occurred, day by day and hour by hour, not after the fact, Dr. Ringelblum himself participated in the collection of data by day and wrote his notes at night.

Fearing the worst after the July 1942 deportations to Treblinka, Dr. Ringelblum gave the signal in early August to bury the first part of the archive in tin boxes. A Yiddish teacher and trusted colleague, along with his two seventeen-year-old assistants, dug the holes and buried the material. Just before sealing the tin boxes, all three included their last wills and testaments. All expressed an awareness of their role in preserving history, uncertainty about their immediate circumstances, and optimism about the fate of the Jewish people.

Additional documents were sealed in milk cans and buried in 1943. A third cache followed. Information pertaining to the murders of the Jews was sent to the Polish underground and was smuggled out of the country, thus showing the world the extent of Nazi atrocities.

Given numerous opportunities to flee, Dr. Ringelblum said, "Not everyone has a right to run away. Someone has to stay behind and lead" (Kassow, "A Stone Under History's Wheel"). In March 1943 he and his family hid in a non-Jewish area in Warsaw. He returned briefly during the Warsaw Ghetto Uprising of April 1943, when he was arrested and sent to a labor camp. Escaping in August 1943, he hid with his wife and son and thirty-four others in an underground bunker in Warsaw, where he worked diligently on a treatise about Polish-Jewish relations. The family's hideout was discovered in March 1944, and he, his wife, and young son were murdered on March 10, 1944.

Dozens and dozens of people—professional historians and laypeople—worked on this archive. Of these dozens, only two survived. In September 1946 one survivor, Hirsch Vasser, helped uncover ten tin boxes housing thousands of documents, and in 1950 Polish construction workers found two big milk cans containing thousands of pages. Many documents have not been recovered.

Dr. Emanuel Ringelblum's son, Uri, d. 1944

NORWAY
SWEDEN
Scotland
NORTH SEA
Northern Ireland
UNITED KINGDOM
IRELAND
DENMARK
Wales
England
Hamburg
Amsterdam
Bergen-Belsen
Berlin
NETHERLANDS
Zbąszyń
GERMANY
ENGLISH CHANNEL
BELGIUM
Buchenwald
Terezin/ Theresienstadt
LUX.
Prague
CZECH REPUBLIC
Paris
Dachau
FRANCE
SWITZERLAND
AUSTRIA
SLOVENIA
CROATIA
ADRIATIC SEA
ITALY
SPAIN
MEDITERRANEAN SEA

Standing in Blood

After Mendel Grossman's photographs from the Łódź Ghetto

Bowl of Soup

This bowl of soup is dear to her—
death, the going price:
potato peels, bones, and broth,
simmered without spice,

peels through guarded ghetto walls,
bones from stolen meat,
heated up and watered down,
barely fit to eat.

Brother does the foraging
to feed the four of them—
he's only nine yet hopes to find
an extra root or stem.

With the spoon from silver chest,
a trace of family's past,
he ladles stock into her bowl
to break the daily fast.

On freezing Warsaw Ghetto days
his broth sustains her soul.
A brother loses childhood here—
it seeps through cracks in bowl.

*Dr. Janusz Korczak walking with his orphans through the Warsaw
Ghetto, August 5, 1942*

His Overtures of Love

Who has not found the heaven below
Will fail of it above.
God's residence is next to mine,
His furniture is love.
     —EMILY DICKINSON

The furnishings are spare at the orphanage
of the Old Doctor from the Radio:
cupboards, chests, cabinets,
moveable curtains to divide
the space by day for classrooms,
reading corner, sewing workshop, club rooms,
the scale to weigh each child.
His furniture is love.

By night partitions drift to make a dormitory
of beds for two hundred children.
Miss Stefa rests in the east end.
In the west, his own bed in the center,
flanked by the beds of the sick children,
posts his Polish military uniform
that he, the proud patriot,
buries under his daily garb
to wear at home and on streets
as he solicits potatoes
and undeliverable packages
from the ghetto post office.
His furniture is love.

Under the bed he stores a bottle of vodka,
black bread, and a jug of water.
On the night table, a fountain pen
and pencils, sharpened at both ends,

wait for his words
when he welcomes "the beautiful
silence of the night."*
His ghetto diary is grim,
unlike his book of the boy-king Matt,
How to Love a Child,
The Child's Right to Respect,
and his other bestsellers.
His signature is love.

Doctor chooses the last
play, *The Post Office*,
for July. It features
sparkling stars circling around
a dying boy, Amal.
"Don't force surprises on the children
if they don't want them."*
"After all, a long dangerous journey
requires preparation."*
His theater is love.

*Janusz Korczak, *Ghetto Diary*.

Timing Is Everything

Feigele, "the little bird," learned early
that timing was everything in the Warsaw Ghetto:
when to teach Jewish children to sing and write,
when to smuggle them over the wall,
when to forge her fate as Vladka,
when to dress dynamite in greasy paper
(call it butter or paint) as vodka
and zlotys prime the Polish guard,
when to carry the map of Treblinka
in her shoes,
when to comfort, tarry, or flee.

Vladka Meed learned later
that her stories, though etched in print and stone,
were best nesting in the hearts
of teachers turned storytellers:
nightmares turned to dreams,
screams to songs,
youth to fighters,
despair to action.

Now, flying higher than this earthly wall,
she rests in peace,
secure that others have glimpsed
the night.

Vladka Meed,
as a Polish girl as pictured on her forged identity card, 1943

History Lessons

Vladka Meed felt more than fame
when she saw her false ID card framed
above her teen granddaughter's bed.
"Stanislawa Wonchalska," it said,
forged and fated to inflame
the ways they fought
in Warsaw Ghetto days—
a granddaughter's highest praise.

Vladka felt the same
when her fourteen-year-old grandson,
asked in history class to name
a woman brave:
"My grandmother," he claimed.
"Can you show she's a real hero?"
"She wrote a very long chapter book."
(He gave the teacher a proper hook.)
"Read it and report to us."
His grade on his report: A-plus.

Chanka Garfinkel, 1946

Chanka Garfinkel: Guarding the Memories

For Helen Greenspun

You may write me down in history
With your bitter, twisted lies,
You may trod me in the very dirt
But still, like dust, I'll rise.
　　　—MAYA ANGELOU

Always the tomboy, town's first girl bike rider,
tree climber, climb higher, Chanka her name,
from Chmielnik the family—five sisters, two brothers—
in Poland swept up and remanded to flame.

Sara, her mother, who treasured the children,
Kalman, her father, an Orthodox Jew,
tried to protect them when *der daytsh* invaded;
they sent Chanka out to a farmer they knew.

With a brother she hid in haystacks of neighbors.
When Germans inspected, she said not a word,
kept milking the cow, did not answer the question,
not wishing the Yiddish of accent be heard.

She returned to her father, hungry but happy,
unshamed by the shearing that marked his disgrace
that tied him to home. The children went scouting,
forced into trucks and young Chanka misplaced.

With Sonia and Nathan to camp she was carted,
Skarżysko-Kamienna for nearly two years.
Her sorting potatoes put food in their stomachs
as theft led to lashes, to facing her fears.

Chanka and Sonia saved food for their brother,
pushing each other to toil, though spent.
She spotted the best place to stand in the soup line
for broth in her blue pot, hands up but head bent.

She stood in the last half of line for roll call;
red paper for rouge was far better than gold.
With passion to live and with prayer to see parents,
though only a teen she was forced to be bold.

She organized ways to conscript what she needed—
rags and ragtag shoes, scraps to survive.
A warden or two looked aside, not reporting;
one managed the factory—is that why she's alive?

This same older guard was sent with the thousands
to Camp Częstochowa to oversee labors.
Though grueling, this camp grimly hosted reunion—
Chanka and four of her siblings were neighbors.

Chanka stole clothing and socks for dear Nathan,
who pleaded with God for his sisters to live:
Regina and Bela, Chanka and Sonia.
An eye, ear, or limb he offered to give.

When Nathan reported to factory work,
a catch of machine nearly cost him his hand.
He's sent on to Buchenwald—girls, Bergen-Belsen;
Chanka prayed painless the gas that was planned.

The thread of life hangs when no food is given,
just skin from potatoes and snow-covered leaf,
shoes lined with the same precious leaves, as unburied
as Chanka and God in their bond of belief.

At Burgau she boarded an airplane to clean it;
she gazed at a satchel of sandwich and fruit.
To eat is to hope against trap and misgiving—
lucky for her there was no looming brute.

To Türkheim, then Dachau, the sisters went marching,
fearing to run through the burstings in air,
Allies above them as they kept on treading,
frozen and sick with no warm coat to wear.

At wit's and the war's end, Chanka with typhus,
the Garfinkel sisters located their brother.
Chanka grew stronger and thrived in DP camp,
sewing and singing the songs of her mother.

der daytsh: the Germans (Yiddish).

Helen Greenspun (Chanka Garfinkel)

Telltale Lines

For Helen Greenspun

If each little line on your face tells a tale,
all stories are here
inscribed for anyone to read:
Mother and Father dreamed a life for each child,
one blessed adventure, the other tradition;
malicious men paraded ambition,
Cain killing Abel six million times;
women, fertile for the fatherland,
traded friendship and kinship
for exiles, famines, and plagues.
Prophets' calls for justice fell silent:
pistols pierced the primeval pine forests,
beasts feasted on pseudoscience,
sadists sang and lorded over their lists.

Nearing death,
you made pacts with yourself.
Brother bargained with God,
sisters nurtured,
soldiers liberated.

After the fire,
you faced the still
small voice
that called,
"Return."

All stories,
a voluminous book,
a cautionary tale.

The cobbler and Norbert Wollheim at Auschwitz,
probably fall 1944

The Standing Prayer

In Memory of Norbert Wollheim

Waiting in line for roll call for hours,
something is wrong; the count is off.
The SS gangsters, no good at figures,
count and recount, time and again.
Yaacov, a cobbler, a pious man,
stands by me, our wretched band;
our heels and soles sink as we stand.

Minutes become hours, hours are weeks,
wind blows off the mountain peaks;
rain pours, the thousands grow weak.
Some who can no longer stand
collapse from the gust of wind and sand.

And Yaacov is praying—
praying, yes, praying.
Yaacov is praying—
praying, yes, praying.

I turn to him, "What are you doing . . . ?
You have said probably
your morning prayers . . ."

    "I am praising God . . .
    Yes, I am thanking Him."

"Are you out of your mind?"*
Psalms and hymns?

Here in Auschwitz, praise seems odd,
yet many of us keep talking to God.

Just like Jacob, Isaac's son,
his wrestling with heaven is already done.

"I'm thanking God
for the fact
that He didn't make me
like the murderers around us."*

I had no response
when he answered thus.

* Norbert Wollheim, Testimony: United States Holocaust
Memorial Museum, February 18, 1992.

Norbert Wollheim at Auschwitz, 1991

No Art

Pausing near the railroad tracks,
Norbert Wollheim, on a teachers' trip,
sits at Auschwitz,
looking back.
Through his mind pictures whip
welded by I. G. Farben's grip,
and retells history,
details, facts:

partings, factory metalwork,
hangings, shootings, betrayals, fears,
shadows where the sadists lurk,
barracks, comrades, brothers, peers,
heads held up
above the jeers,
birth dates changed as *der Blockschreiber*, clerk.

He recalls debarking from the train
when his family arrived
and stands where commands of Cain
left him forever twice deprived—
his wife, his son, just he survived,
a daily
dose of pain.

Ready to depart,
this gentle man recounts, relives,
teaches with a stalwart heart
the story that he freely gives,
says will and luck
are why he lives—
survival is no art.

der Blockschreiber: the barracks clerk, secretary, record keeper
(German).

Leibke Kaganowicz

Patzan

Leibke Kaganowicz from Eishyshok,
a gentle guide with a shepherd's crook,
drove sheep from Radun to the eastern front
while Lithuanians played
a game of murder.
"I must leave, Papa," his dark eyes pled.
Beckoned by birch trees,
Leibke fled.

Hidden with brother Benjamin
in the Catholic cemetery, he had seen
the end of all their life had been—
Eishyshok.

Defenders called him *patzan*, boy;
the tender street name brought him joy.
The forest lent no time to mourn
Grandmother, Father, Sister, Brother.
He still remembers leaving
Mother.

Light-footed as a shepherd lad,
he gathered food for the *otriad*.
Russians taught to hold a rifle,
explode supplies meant for Prussians,
melt and bend tracks like spaghetti,
plant English mines when they were ready.
Their best refrains were derailed trains—
dynamite, their fantastic chorus.

When wartime ended in the forest,
Leibke, nineteen, was newly old,
no longer labeled young *patzan*,
but bold and seasoned partisan.

patzan: boy, lad (Russian slang).
otriad: official partisan detachment (Russian).

The poet Abraham Sutzkever...

...as a partisan in Vilna

Abraham Sutzkever in Vilna

"Unter dayne vayse shtern": A Sonnet for Sutzkever

At night I look through darkened doors ajar
for Mama. I (the pitted plum that bears
within the nest, the bird, the tree) have fears
that wagons cart her Sabbath shoes to war.
I wait for Your white hand beneath Your star
to stretch through snowy night and hold my tears;
from cellared holes, dear God, I search the years
past rooftops where Your shelter stands afar.

By night we raid the printer's plates of lead
that once engraved the Golden Chain's old script.
For arms, we melt the ingrained voice of scrolls
while dreamers, turned to soldiers, forge ahead.
We sing a hymn to swamps once nondescript;
we shoulder sacred rifles on our souls.

"Unter dayne vayse shtern": "Beneath Your White Stars"
(Yiddish), the title of a well-known poem by Abraham Sutzkever.

Abraham Sutzkever as a young poet in Vilna

Sutzkever's Stars

In the silence of the night
I rise to stanzas of his light,
the spine of stars, Orion's belt,
a glowing ring of what he felt.
Stars knew of Egypt's famined grain,
like words, restored in sheaves again.
His fallen star, a newborn child,
could live through him when strophes were styled.
Whitened stars fell into tears
as meter marked his earthly fears.
He wished for embryonic times
when stars were watered by his rhyme.
From afar he sang of dust,
the steady stars a heart could trust.
The candles counted heaven's space,
cantillations at his pace.

Nesa Galperin in Šiauliai, Lithuania

L'Chaim

For Nesse Godin

My eyes will sign a hasty match
that Mama strikes from her wise heart.
A husband quickly she will catch.

Our family had been torn apart,
expelled from home to hostile land.
From nothing, fire is hard to start.

The cling of need predicts a plan
that one of us must race to wed.
We need the brace of a good man.

She chooses me—I can't be led
from spring's remains to winter's year,
so Yankel, young, she picks instead.

A glance reveals he seems my peer
of striking looks; I find him fair.
Behalf beholds, she draws him near.

A "yes" from Yankel makes the pair.
At seventeen I sing the pride
of circumstance; they raise my chair,

L'Chaim from places where we died.
Mazel—seventy years a bride.

L'Chaim: to life (Hebrew).
Mazel: luck, good luck (Hebrew).

Tousia Goldberg (Tess Wise) in Szydłowiec

A Glezele Tei

For Tess Wise, July 2015

Shimmering gold, Tess invites
me to stay for tea and crumpets.
Brewing for four o'clock,
the time they took tea in Poland,
she pours, as in the past.
Even schooldays at the Jewish gymnasium
meant large meals at midday
between Latin, German, Hebrew,
and Polish literature,
mathematics and science.
Her books from their cases, open,
fresh-read in French,
she is eager for table talk
of poets from her youth:
the lyrical Latin of Catullus and Lucretius,
the Germans Goethe, Schiller, and Rilke,
the French bards,
the medieval Hebrew masters
and Jews who loved Zion in rhyme.
Her mother, too, knew foreign tongues,
and corners of her girlhood home in Szydłowiec
cradled Yiddish books.
Tess brings an encyclopedia to share
words about her grandfather great,
a chief rabbi of Poland,
himself a linguist—
Hebrew for prayer and study,
Yiddish for everyday,
Polish for his place in Parliament,
Russian to hail the ascension of the Czar.
Bearded and traditional,
he walked in the world,

a Polish patriot,
helping the *kehilla*.
Tess is still their child,
steeped in tradition,
holding tea, poetry, and community
in her shining heart.

Tess Wise

a glezele tei: a glass of tea (Yiddish).
kehilla: a Jewish community (Hebrew).

Lost and *Found*

Jewish woman in a ghetto in Poland, 1942

Bowl of Soup

Since the Germans allotted just several hundred calories of food per day to each Jew, hunger was a constant problem in the ghettos. In the Warsaw Ghetto children frequently risked their lives to smuggle food to feed their families, their small bodies crawling through barbed wire or squeezing through holes in ghetto walls under the eyes of the German authorities. Documents and diaries from Warsaw and many other ghettos recorded this daily struggle.

Mendel Grossman (1913–1945), the photographer of the Łódź Ghetto Council, hid his camera beneath his coat and illegally took more than ten thousand photographs, including one of a brother feeding his little sister in the Łódź Ghetto, an image that inspired this poem. On December 8, 1941, Mordechai Chaim Rumkowski, the head of the *Judenrat* (a Jewish council that was appointed to carry out the directives of the Germans in the ghetto), prohibited Mendel Grossman from taking photographs for "private purposes." Despite pleas from family and friends, he continued to photograph life and death in Łódź.

His Overtures of Love

Janusz Korczak (1878–1942), the pen name of Henryk Goldszmit, was a Jewish pediatrician, educator, writer, and champion of children who devoted his whole career in Poland to studying and nurturing children. From 1912 to 1942 he served as the director of the Jewish Orphans' Home in Warsaw, and he founded an institute for Catholic children in 1919. He studied childhood and adapted his psychological findings for educators and parents. The author of twenty-four books for adults and children, he trained teachers in moral education, worked in juvenile courts defending children's rights, and appeared on his own radio program in the mid- to late '30s. He advocated treating children with the utmost respect and modeled his orphanage on these principles. Throughout Poland and particularly in his beloved Warsaw, he was very highly regarded by his Jewish and non-Jewish audiences.

When World War II broke out, he remained in Warsaw, though he was offered refuge because of his reputation. At the time of the Warsaw Ghetto his orphanage housed two hundred Jewish children, and he guided other institutions that assisted destitute children of other faiths. He and his very devoted staff, including Stefania Wilczynska, who worked with him for thirty years, tended the children of the ghetto with great affection and care. As his diary reveals, he spent most of his time procuring food and other resources and administering medical care and emotional support for the children. Anticipating the worst, Dr. Korczak selected the play performed by the children in July 1942, Tagore's *The Post Office*, to help the terrified children accept death more serenely.

When the Nazis rounded up Dr. Korczak, his staff, and his two hundred children at the orphanage on August 5, 1942, he marched for miles with his children in an orderly manner to the trains, each of his hands holding the hand of a child. He had again refused offers of refuge; he would not abandon the children who loved and trusted him. He could not save them, but he was their only comfort and remained so until the end. He died with all his children at Treblinka.

The pioneering educational work of Janusz Korczak is still widely celebrated in Poland and in Israel. Both locations host kite festivals inspired by a statement from his *The Religion of the Child*: "Just as the sea gives a child a toy—a boat, so the wind has to give him a kite."

A Jewish girl in Warsaw

Timing Is Everything
History Lessons

Vladka Meed (1921–2012), born Feigele Peltel in a district of Warsaw, served as a courier of arms and information in the Warsaw Ghetto. A member of the Jewish Labor Bund at the age of fourteen, she joined the newly created Jewish Coordinating Committee, which soon focused on the needs of the Żydowska Organizacja Bojowa, or ŻOB (Jewish Fighting Organization), in the Warsaw Ghetto. Successfully posing as a Gentile with her flawless Polish and light hair, she was smuggled to the "Aryan side" of the wall, dropping her Yiddish name, Feigele ("little bird"), for the Polish nickname Vladka, which she retained even after liberation. She purchased bullets, pistols, and dynamite and carried them to the Jewish side of the wall by pretending to be part of a Polish work detail, bribing her way across or climbing over the wall. At a time when there was still uncertainty about the function of Treblinka, she carried a map of the death camp to the underground. On several occasions she smuggled Jewish children to the "Aryan side" for safekeeping.

On Both Sides of the Wall (1948) is her account of these experiences, one of the first eyewitness reports of resistance in the Warsaw Ghetto. Her false identity card is on display at the United States Holocaust Memorial Museum, and as she reported in her testimony for the Shoah Foundation, her granddaughter proudly posted a facsimile above her bed. Here she also told of her grandson reading her story in *On Both Sides of the Wall.*

After the war she and her husband, Benjamin Meed, also a courier for the underground in Warsaw, devoted much of their energy to helping Holocaust survivors and to celebrating Yiddish culture in the United States. Both became leaders of the survivor community with Benjamin Meed starting and heading the American Gathering of Holocaust Survivors for many years. In the mid-1980s Vladka Meed worked with the American Federation of Teachers, the Jewish Labor Committee, and the American Gathering of Jewish Holocaust Survivors to train teachers in Holocaust education. For many years she herself led the teachers through Warsaw, the death camps in German-occupied Poland, Yad Vashem, and the Ghetto Fighters' House Museum. More than seven hundred teachers participated in her program of study, this poet among them, and we call ourselves "Vladka's teachers."

Chanka Garfinkel: Guarding the Memories
Telltale Lines

Helen Greenspun (b. 1926) is a Holocaust survivor who has lived in the Orlando area since 1973. For decades she has spoken regularly to thousands of schoolchildren in Central Florida about life before the war in a small town in Poland and of existence in labor and concentration camps in Poland and Germany from 1942 through 1945. Her listeners are surprised to hear of her life in a displaced persons camp in Germany for several years after the war. She and four of her siblings survived years of Nazi camp life, and *Sara's Children and the Destruction of Chmielnik*, by Suzan E. Hagstrom, chronicles her story. Helen speaks for her girlfriends who did not survive and in memory of her parents and two youngest siblings, who were murdered by the Nazis.

Throughout her lifetime Helen has been known by several names. Her Yiddish name is Chana, and her parents affectionately called her Chaneleh. Her Polish name is Chanka, and many of her schoolmates and fellow laborers called her by that name. In the United States she is usually known with great affection as Helen.

Standing Prayer
No Art

Norbert Wollheim (1913–1998) of Berlin began his studies to become an attorney after graduating from high school in 1931, but he realized that he would not be permitted to have a career in law in Germany. Instead, he did volunteer work with the Jewish community and in 1935 began working for a Jewish firm that traded in iron and manganese ore. When an unusual opportunity to help the Jewish community arose, Norbert directed his considerable energy to help administer the *Kindertransport*. He found escorts for the children, communicated with parents who were sending their children away and with adults who were taking the children in, and served as an escort himself on some of the train trips. His talent as an organizer had manifested in Jewish youth group work, and he used this gift, along with his passion to help the Jewish children, to move thousands to safety.

After the start of war, when emigration became very difficult, Norbert trained to work as a welder and worked in this field until March 1943, when he, his wife, and their three-year-old child were arrested and deported to Auschwitz. His wife and son were immediately sent to the gas chamber, and Norbert was placed in Buna/Monowitz, a subcamp of Auschwitz, for forced labor. In June 1943 he worked as a welder with other skilled metalworkers at the I. G. Farben factory at Buna/Monowitz. He was able to help fellow prisoners by altering penciled birth dates on documents to make aging men appear to be younger and thus more suitable candidates for work. He befriended many, including the pious cobbler Yaacov, who prayed while they were standing for hours at *Appell* (roll call). His friends included British prisoners of war who provided supplies and information that kept up his morale.

Just prior to the liberation of Auschwitz by the Red Army, Norbert and the other prisoners of Auschwitz were marched in a final evacuation of the camp in January 1945. Temperatures were freezing, and they were starving. In April 1945 he and several fellow prisoners fled and were finally freed in Schwerin, Germany, by American soldiers.

Serving as the chairman of the Central Committee of Liberated Jews in the British Zone in Germany, Norbert Wollheim brought awareness of displaced persons and other Holocaust victims. For several years he helped rebuild the Jewish community in Germany, although he and his new wife made plans to leave.

Norbert Wollheim

In the interim, Norbert served as a witness in several postwar trials, including the 1947 I. G. Farben trial in Nuremberg and the 1949 trial in Hamburg of Veit Harlan, the director of a wildly popular antisemitic film shown in wartime Germany. Norbert testified about the devastating effects of this film on the Jewish community and addressed the failure of the postwar German courts to take action. As he predicted, the courts found Harlan not guilty of any crime, and this verdict hastened Norbert's departure from Germany. In the first case of this type he sued I. G. Farben in Frankfurt Regional Court in 1951 for compensation as a slave laborer. The court ruled in his favor, requiring the company to pay him for his time as a worker. This case set a precedent for compensating other slave laborers as well.

Immigrating to the United States in 1951, he studied accounting and worked in this profession until the 1990s. He devoted much energy to the survivor community and to Holocaust education. Norbert Wollheim accompanied us on our teachers' trip to Poland and to Israel to study the Holocaust. At Auschwitz and later in Israel he shared the facts, stories, and emotions related in these two poems.

In 1996 the state of Hesse, Germany, acquired the I. G. Farben Building, the headquarters for the company and the site where wartime decisions to cooperate with the National Socialist regime were made. The building became part of the campus of Goethe University in Frankfurt. The controversial history of the building is featured prominently, and on November 2, 2008, the Norbert Wollheim Memorial opened on these grounds to commemorate the prisoners who worked for I. G. Farben at Buna/Monowitz. On the outside of the memorial pavilion, the number 107984 stands boldly, the prisoner number for Norbert Wollheim. Inside the pavilion his quote from August 26, 1945, introduces the complexity of survival: "We have been saved, but we are not liberated."

Patzan

Leon Kahn (1925–2003), born Leibke Kaganowicz, became a partisan as a young teenager. Normal life ceased for Leibke and his close-knit family in Eishyshok, Lithuania, with the arrival of the *Einsatzgruppen*, German mobile killing squads comprised of SS and German police, usually accompanied by local collaborators. On September 25, 1941, the *Einsatzgruppen* and Lithuanian shooters rounded up the Jewish men and killed most of them; the women and children met the same fate the following day. Leibke reported that approximately five thousand were brutally murdered in these two days, including nearly one thousand children. He and his older brother witnessed the killings while hiding in a nearby Catholic cemetery.

The Kaganowicz family escaped to the Radun Ghetto, where Leibke herded two thousand sheep onto a train that was headed to the eastern front. On this assignment the Lithuanians made sport of killing as many Jews as they could. The escape to Radun provided only a short-lived refuge; most of Radun's Jews were murdered at the hands of the *Einsatzgruppen* and collaborators on May 10, 1942. Again, the Kaganowicz family survived this massacre, this time by hiding in a cellar.

What should be their next move? Leibke expressed the desire to run to the forest, but his father was not sure this was the best strategy. Leibke's father and two siblings left Radun to hide with acquaintances. His mother refused to consider moving to the forest, unwilling to abandon her own elderly mother. After a few more makeshift attempts to survive in different places and just narrowly avoiding being taken to Auschwitz from Grodno in January 1943, Leibke convinced his father that he must leave. He joined with a Russian partisan group under the command of Lieutenant Anton Stankevich and as one of the youngest members of the group was called *patzan*, a slang term for a boy.

As a partisan, Leibke was trained in guerilla warfare, specializing in railway sabotage, blowing up trains on their way to the eastern front, thus depriving the German army of food and other supplies. His responsibilities in the *otriad* also included securing food for the unit. They had many successful missions, and he described the experience of blowing up an enemy train as fantastic because his unit was doing something to help win the war.

His father, brother, and sister stayed with a partisan group in the forest. Leibke's brother, Benjamin, wanted to join him but needed a weapon for admission to the Russian partisans. Benjamin was killed in the process of obtaining this weapon. Leibke's father and sister, Friedke, were intentionally attacked and killed by the Polish Home Army, the AK, whose primary mission was to fight Nazis. His mother and grandmother were caught up in the Nazi web and died at Treblinka.

Leibke Kaganowicz moved to Canada after the war, taking the name Leon Kahn. In Vancouver he became a successful businessman, community leader, philanthropist, and devoted family man.

"Unter dayne vayse shtern": A Sonnet for Sutzkever
Sutzkever's Stars

Abraham (Avrom) Sutzkever (1913–2010) fought the Nazis first with his pen and then with weapons. Born near Vilna, he spent his earliest days in Siberia, where the snowy landscape furnished ready images to his young mind. After the death of his father at age thirty, Abraham returned with his mother and siblings to Vilna, the "Jerusalem of Lithuania," where he lived between the world wars. Tragedy struck again when his sister died of meningitis.

When he was thirteen, he started writing poetry, at least partly to remember his father and sister. Initially self-educated, he welded the nuances of his treasured Yiddish with modern and classical themes and poetic forms. In poetry he discovered something that could conquer death. He lived for a time in Warsaw, and his first book was published there by the Yiddish Writers' Union. When World War II broke out, he married Freydke, another admirer of poetry and Yiddish culture.

Abraham Sutzkever

Germany attacked the Soviet Union on June 22, 1941, and reached Vilna two days later. More than one hundred thousand Jews of Vilna and the provinces would be murdered in the forests of nearby Ponary. Most of the surviving Jews were placed in a ghetto, but Sutzkever hid in a tiny crawl space in his mother's apartment and in other places. He was caught on September 5, 1941, and lined up to be shot, but the Lithuanians sent him to the newly established ghetto instead. Here he stayed until September 1943.

Sutzkever was entrenched in the cultural life of the Vilna Ghetto (1941–1943), writing and teaching Yiddish poetry and songs to the youth. He believed that only through poetry would he survive the Holocaust, and he wished to share this life-giving art with youth. His long poem "The Grave Child" earned the 1942 literary prize of the Ghetto Writers' Union. He searched for God in "Unter dayne vayse shtern" ("Beneath Your White Stars"), a poem that was set to music by Avrom Brudno and became one of the most popular songs in the Vilna Ghetto. His mother disappeared in the ghetto; he wrote of his search for her in "My Mother" and of the carting away of her precious Sabbath shoes in "A Wagon of Shoes." In "The Lead Plates of the Rom Printers," Sutzkever revealed a projected plan to forge bullets by melting down lead plates of the Rom Press, a distinguished printing house known for its beautiful editions of the Babylonian Talmud and other religious books. The letters, once the building blocks of sacred texts, would become bullets to preserve life itself.

Sutzkever connected with a group of young people and intellectuals who worked outside the ghetto walls at YIVO, an institute founded in Vilna in 1925 to preserve, teach, and study the history of Jewish life in Russia, Germany, and eastern Europe with a focus on Yiddish-language materials. Under the Nazis these young people were forced to collect Yiddish and Hebrew resources for the proposed "Institute for the Study of the Jewish Question," and books were to be shipped to Frankfurt, Germany, or sent to a paper factory. Instead, he and his colleagues, including the poet and partisan Abba Kovner, risked their lives by smuggling treasured books into the ghetto library or by burying them.

YIVO was also the site where weapons were smuggled to the underground and then made their way into the ghetto. Here he and fellow poet Shmerke Kaczerginski received the first machine gun for the United Partisan Organization.

On September 12, 1943, Sutzkever, his wife, Kaczerginski, and other YIVO workers who were partisans escaped from the Vilna Ghetto to nearby forests. They made forays from the forests to Vilna to save Jews who had survived the failed ghetto uprising. Sutzkever joined the Voroshilov Brigade under Fiodor Markov in the Naroch Forest. Here he kept records of testimonies of Nazi crimes and of the partisan activity in the area. A big hunt by the Nazis left many fighters dead, but the Sutzkevers and Kaczerginski survived and were soon summoned by Markov to write the account of partisan activity.

In swamps and forests Sutzkever continued to compose poetry. He wrote "To My Wife" about the poisoning of their infant son by the Nazis in the ghetto. He lauded the sanctuary of the marsh in "March Through Swamps," describing partisans carrying the wounded on their shoulders.

Surprisingly, a cable from Moscow specified that a plane would be sent to airlift Abraham and Freydke Sutzkever from German-occupied land. Partisans had carried his poems about the horrors of Nazi handiwork to Moscow, where they had made a strong impression. The president of the Lithuanian government in exile in Moscow, himself a poet, had also translated some of Sutzkever's poems in 1940. He remembered the poet and saved him. The couple finally reached Moscow in March 1944, and the Soviet journal *Pravda* reported his account of the Holocaust and of the tenacity of Jewish resisters.

With the liberation of Vilna in July, Sutzkever returned to the city. Abba Kovner and Shmerke Kaczerginski, fellow partisans and poets, participated in liberating Vilna and digging up the buried cultural treasures. Sutzkever was selected to serve as a witness at the Nuremberg trials of 1946.

He and Freydke illegally left for Palestine (the land that would later become Israel) in 1947. He continued writing poetry in Yiddish and established the Yiddish literary quarterly, *Di goldene keyt* (*The Golden Chain*). He was its sole editor from its inception in 1949 through 1996. It featured work by Yiddish writers from around the world and art by prominent Jewish artists. Marc Chagall, his lifelong friend, contributed drawings and Yiddish poems to the journal.

Abraham Sutzkever has been acclaimed as one of the greatest poets of the Holocaust and one of the finest Yiddish poets of the twentieth century.

L'Chaim

Nesse Godin (Nesa), born in 1928 to Pinchas and Sara Galperin, lived in Šiauliai, Lithuania, with her parents and two older brothers, Yechezkel and Menashe, in a religious and close-knit family. Life changed with the occupation of Šiauliai by the German army on June 26, 1941, with several thousand Jews murdered in the forest and the remaining five thousand, including her family, forced into a ghetto. From this ghetto her father was deported to Auschwitz and gassed immediately.

With the German liquidation of the Šiauliai Ghetto in July 1944, all surviving residents were sent to camps in Germany, German-annexed lands, or Poland. Nesa, Yechezkel, and their mother, Sara, were deported; Nesa and her mother were sent to Stutthof in north central Poland but were in different subcamps. From here Nesa was sent to four other camps and on a death march in January 1945. She credits older women for giving her advice and encouragement to survive and recounts how they requested to be remembered if she lived. After liberation by the Soviet army on March 10, 1945, she spent six weeks healing in a hospital and, upon her release, was assigned a young foster mother. Together they went to Łódź, Poland, where many survivors were assembled. Here she received news that her mother was alive, and she left to find Sara.

After their reunion, Sara quickly determined that one of them needed to marry for economic reasons. At forty-six, Sara announced that she would not marry again; Nesa would be the one.

At age seventeen Nesa did not understand why this was necessary since they had each other. And whom would she marry? Sara proceeded to scout out the prospects where survivors had gathered. Nesa herself had evaluated the potential candidates and rejected her mother's first picks, one thirty years older than she. Yankel, a younger man who was later called Jack, responded positively when Sara asked if he would marry her daughter. He agreed and took hold of Nesa's hand to request that she become his bride. She looked to her mother, who was nodding. A match was made, and in August 1945, she and Yankel married in a civil ceremony.

Nesa, Yankel, and Sara proceeded to the American zone of Germany and lived in a displaced persons camp in Feldafing. Here Nesa and Jack had a second wedding, a religious ceremony,

Wedding gown sewn from a parachute

on May 2, 1946. They started their family at this camp, where they lived until immigrating in 1950 to America, settling in the Washington, DC, area where they currently reside.

I met Nesse Godin, a volunteer at the United States Holocaust Memorial Museum, while I was visiting an exhibit on life in the displaced persons camp. As I looked at an unusual flowing dress, she explained that many brides had worn downed parachutes refashioned into wedding gowns. She was quite the expert on weddings and spoke warmly of her own marriage. With her work she intentionally honors the women who helped her to survive.

A Glezele Tei

Tess Wise is a survivor from Poland who for decades has been passionate about Holocaust education. Born Tousia Goldberg in a small town near Radom called Szydłowiec, she was encouraged by her parents to embrace music, languages, literature, and Judaism. Her great-grandfather Rabbi Abraham Tsevi Perlmutter (1844/46–1930) was likewise a linguist. As the head rabbi of Radom, he delivered an eloquent address in Russian when Nicholas II became tsar in 1896. In 1902, as chief rabbi of Warsaw, he served the Jewish community and wrote texts on Jewish law. His fluency in Polish allowed him to work with the Polish government during the German occupation in World War I and later as an elected representative in the Polish parliament, where he was known for his patriotic speeches delivered in Polish.

When Tousia was a teenager, she moved to Radom, where she attended a private high school, the "Friends of Knowledge" Gymnasium. There she studied Latin, German, French, Hebrew, Polish, and their respective literary works. With the start of war and the occupation of Poland, Jewish schools, including hers, were closed immediately. In 1941 her family moved into a ghetto in Radom. They were sent to a nearby labor camp, where they worked in a munitions factory, and there her mother died of pneumonia.

Tess's father wanted her to flee from the labor camp. In the spring of 1942, a non-Jewish friend and former neighbor named Maria, who worked at the camp office, covertly brought extra civilian clothes to work. Tess dressed in these civilian clothes and walked with her friend through the front gate of the camp. Tess made her way to a town near Lublin and lived under a false identity until the area was liberated by the Soviets in the fall of 1944.

After the liberation of Radom in May 1945, Tess reunited with the only surviving members of her father's family: four of her father's thirteen siblings and her favorite cousin. Faced with hostility and violence in Poland, the family moved to Germany, and Tess attended medical school at the University of Munich. In 1947 she immigrated to the United States upon the invitation of an American uncle who had homes in New Jersey and in Orlando, Florida.

In Orlando, she took the name Tess and learned to speak English while training for an administrative job. She met Abe Wise, who became her husband in 1949, and they started a family and quickly became leaders in the Jewish community. Later Tess received a master's degree in French literature.

Driven by her dream of a society free from antisemitism and all other kinds of bigotry, in the late 1970s she envisioned the idea for a Holocaust center, and under her leadership the first Holocaust resource and education center of its kind in the Southeast was established in Maitland, Florida, in the early 1980s. Its mission stressed educating the community and training teachers to instruct in the field. In 2006 and 2007 Tess initiated "Project Poland" and started a summer institute designed to help Polish schoolteachers gain competency to teach the Holocaust. The annual institute convenes at the Jagiellonian University in Kraków, where a doctoral program in Holocaust Studies is now offered. Currently Tess serves as the chairman of the board of the Holocaust Memorial Resource and Education Center of Florida, the organization that she founded.

Rabbi Abraham Tsevi Perlmutter, Tess's great-grandfather

NORWAY
SWEDEN
Scotland
NORTH SEA
Northern Ireland
UNITED KINGDOM
IRELAND
DENMARK
Wales
England
Hamburg
Schwerin
Bergen-Belsen
Berlin
NETHERLANDS
GERMANY
ENGLISH CHANNEL
BELGIUM
Buchenwald
Frankfurt
LUX.
Nuremberg
CZECH REPUBLIC
Burgau
Dachau
Türkheim
Munich
Feldafing
FRANCE
AUSTRIA
SWITZERLAND
SLOVENIA
CROATIA
ADRIATIC SEA
ITALY
SPAIN
MEDITERRANEAN SEA

* Showing present-day borders

FINLAND

ESTONIA

LATVIA

RUSSIA

Moscow

BALTIC
SEA

Šiauliai

LITHUANIA

Naroch
Forest

Vilna

RUSSIA Eishyshok

Stutthof

Radun

Grodno

BELARUS

POLAND

Treblinka

Warsaw

Łódź

Radom

Szydłowiec

Lublin

Skarżysko-Kamienna

Częstochowa

Chmielnik

Kraków

Auschwitz

UKRAINE

SLOVAKIA

MOLDOVA

HUNGARY

ROMANIA

BLACK SEA

BOSNIA
AND
HERZ.

SERBIA

MONT.

KOSOVO

BULGARIA

MACEDONIA

ALBANIA

GREECE

AEGEAN
SEA

TURKEY

Rescue

Chiune Sugihara

Mr. Sugihara's Eyes

Through the window Mr. Sugihara spies
a sea of pleading eyes behind the gate;
he sees their lives rest solely in his hands.
The Japanese government first denies
their pleas; escape for these will come too late
unless they leave at once for foreign lands.

To Curaçao, the Dutch open their doors;
for Jews in Kovno, the world's a spinning wheel,
rotating them to Vladivostok, then Japan,
needing visas to depart for distant shores.
Thrice Mr. Sugihara wires appeal;
thrice Tokyo halts the motion of his plan.

With furrowed brow and tired, sleepless eyes
the consul weighs which law he will obey;
his hand can save them with his pen—
for transit visa each man in line applies.
He sees there's not a moment to delay,
transfixed by gravity of Jewish men.

Inspired by Mother's roots as samurai?
His school in Harbin taught "Do much for others,
expect little in return" (his school creed).*
Linguistic prowess makes the perfect spy
who sees these men outside the gate as brothers.
Armed with honor, his pen will do the deed.

Steadied by Yukiko, his brave wife,
he signs a passage for each one in line
to Russia's edge, to Kobe, then Shanghai?
For weeks he handwrites visas saving life—
two thousand and one hundred thirty-nine,
the measure of the righteous man's reply.

*Motto of the Harbin Gakuin National University in
Manchuria, China ("Sugihara: Conspiracy of Kindness").

Yukiko and Chiune Sugihara in Kovno, Lithuania, summer 1940

Father Bruno Reynders with some of his rescued children in Belgium,
1943

Kissing the Wall

Jack Goldstein boarded the train
to Maaseik, Belgium, northeast bound,
under the cloak of Father Bruno.
Hide-and-seek Father allowed
though hiding Jews was no game now—
false IDs, food ration cards,
white-robed Jewish boys on guard,
new last names, new faith taught,
Hebrew prayers in Jack's throat caught,
sardines on Sunday with oil-dipped bread,
the convent's children equally fed,
reunion with Mother because of Father,
Father Bruno (Henri Reynders).

Rachelle Silberman, placed by Father
in Bruges, Belgium, near the North Sea,
in a convent of Franciscan sisters
carried a blue coat she called *mon ami*
for cold bare knees of convent school,
steely rows of kneeling stools.
Others spoke with lighted eyes—
"Before the War"—that paradise.
"My parents are coming . . . My parents are here"*
because of the kindness of Father, Père.

Flora Mendelowicz of Brussels
was sent by her mother, entrusted to him
who biked in disguise, crisscrossing through Belgium
to hide Jewish children, spinning a hymn.
Dom dressed the part of six different people,
his shorn head hidden, a beret he wore;
he stole ration cards feeding hundreds of children,
recycled as orphans or through convent doors.

The whir of his wheels moved Flora again
to Our Lady of Seven Sorrows; she thrived,
thanks to the sisters and thanks to Father,
the Benedictine, who kept the hive.

Our guide at the US museum is Flora,
who points to his name in the Rescuers' Hall.
He was "a saint if ever there was one,"†
Abbé Bruno Reynders—
she kisses the wall.

*Rachelle Silberman Goldstein (Greenfeld).
†Flora Mendelowicz Singer (Testimony, *First Person* series).

*Flora Mendelowicz Singer at the Rescuers' Wall at the United States
Holocaust Memorial Museum*

Raoul Wallenberg

The Likeness of a Man

For Raoul Wallenberg (1912–?)

You always were an archangel on wheels,
honed honesty and love from youthful days.
You mobilized your strength from your ideals.

The Swedish diplomat Grandfather feels
that grooming for a higher calling pays.
You always were an archangel on wheels.

In Michigan, architecture appeals;
your public housing projects earn high praise.
You mobilized your strength from your ideals.

You map your blueprints for life-saving deals,
protecting Jews in houses and railways.
You always were an archangel on wheels.

For Jews in Budapest your passport seals;
three golden crowns: a *Schutzpass* boldly says
you mobilized your strength from your ideals.

The ledger, tossed in leather case, reveals
the dispatched host who exits in a haze—
You always were an archangel on wheels.
You mobilized your strength from your ideals.

Schutzpass: Schutz means protection; *pass,* passport (German).

Jewish girl hidden at a convent school at her first Communion

A Crowd of Hosts

The heavens are the heavens of the Lord
and the earth He has given to humankind.
—PSALM 115:16

When the host, army at the threshold,
stole inside the house,
Jews, "parasites" of the German host
and in lands the Germans grabbed,
saw no host of heavenly angels
hoisting them to safety.
Not starry-eyed,
this host of dusty sparrows
searched for a corner,
a nest near the ground,
muting their music,
quieting song,
seeking sanctuary in secret
places of well-lit souls.
If Father or Sister spared them
from the Arrow Cross or Thunder Cross
or hid their children, for whom host
was bread, not body,
the Golden Rule had tendered
upright sentinels,
who, a rising host of daffodils,
trumpeted at sunrise.

Arrow Cross: Fascist group in Hungary.
Thunder Cross: collaborationist paramilitary organization
in Latvia.

Risen and Rescued

Recipes for Jewish holiday bread disappeared—
gone are the round Russian challahs topped with ladders
lifting and leaning toward the Lord;
gone are Ukrainian breads shaped like birds
who hover over their fledglings
just as God takes Jerusalem under His wing;
gone are Lithuanian loaves crusted with crowns,
honoring God with their golden baked orbs.
Yet, with their bakers, some recipes survived;
from Cologne, the six-braided Russian strands
made their exodus to new Promised Lands,
designed and entwined,
risen and rescued.

Lost and *Found*

Mr. Sugihara's Eyes

Chiune (Sempo) Sugihara (1900–1986) was the Japanese consul general sent to Kovno, Lithuania, in the fall of 1939 to monitor German and Russian troop movements near Lithuania's borders. Fluent in Russian, German, Chinese, English, French, and Japanese, he was uniquely prepared for this assignment.

After the German invasion of Poland in September 1939, many Polish Jews fled to nearby Lithuania for safety. But when the Soviet Union annexed Lithuania in June 1940, Lithuania ceased to be a haven. The Russians ordered foreign consulates to close, and a German invasion seemed imminent. On July 27, 1940, Chiune Sugihara found hundreds of Jews assembled at the gate of his office. They needed his help to leave the country, but where could they go?

The Dutch colony of Curaçao was open to refugees according to the acting Dutch consul in Lithuania, Jan Zwartendijk. How could the Jewish refugees reach Curaçao? A possible trajectory included leaving Kovno by rail, proceeding through Russia to Vladivostok on the coast, and then to Kobe, Japan, by sea. Jews with "Curaçao visas" would need transit visas to travel through Japan to reach Curaçao. Chiune Sugihara was ready to write the documents, but the Japanese government rejected his request three times. However, with encouragement from his wife, Yukiko, he acted on his own and wrote the visas against the directive of his government.

From late July to late August 1940, Chiune Sugihara handwrote 2,139 visas. Each visa allowed an entire family to flee, and more than six thousand Jews escaped. Most visa recipients were adult males—leaders of organized religious or political groups, businessmen, lawyers, and journalists—who were considered to be at high risk if they remained in eastern Europe. About half of these escaping Polish Jews went from Kobe to Shanghai, some right away and some when they were later sent by the Japanese government. An entire Lithuanian yeshiva (an academy for advanced religious studies) was relocated to Shanghai through Mr. Sugihara's efforts. The other half of the Polish refugees had no certain path from Japan, and some eventually settled in the United States, Canada, and Palestine (the land that would later become Israel).

According to Sugihara's son, the Jews were filled with gratitude for his work, saying, "We will never forget you. We will see you again." After writing the visa for each individual, the consul looked the recipient in the eye and wished him good luck (Mochizuki). In late summer 1940, Chiune Sugihara and his family were ordered to leave Kovno to report to Berlin. As he was departing, he was still writing visas from his hotel and from the train. After a temporary stay in Berlin and Czechoslovakia, the Sugiharas were posted to Königsberg, Germany, and finally to Romania.

In 1945 the diplomat and his family were imprisoned in a Soviet internment camp for more than one year. The Sugiharas finally arrived in Japan in spring 1947. Several months later the Japanese ministry asked him to resign. After doing menial work he took a job with a trading company in Moscow using the name Sempo, a Sino-Japanese form of his name, as a way to remain unrecognized since he was no favorite of the government of the Soviet Union.

A Belgian nun who rescued Jewish children,
after a photograph from Father Bruno's nephew Michel Reynders

Many Jews who survived because of his visas tried to locate him, and in 1968 one succeeded. The Israeli government brought Chiune Sugihara to visit Israel. He had not spoken of his work to anyone and sought no accolades, in keeping with the mission of public service that he had been taught while attending school in Harbin. In Jerusalem in 1985 he was honored as one of the "Righteous Among the Nations," an award given by the state of Israel to non-Jews who saved one or more Jews during the Holocaust. Although Sugihara was too ill to attend the ceremony, Yukiko and their oldest son accepted the award on his behalf, and a tree was planted at Yad Vashem in his honor. In 1992 the "Hill of Humanity" was built in his hometown of Yaotsu, Japan, a belated acknowledgment of his humanitarian achievement.

The name "Chiune" means "one thousand furrows."

Kissing the Wall

Reverend Henri Reynders, also known as Father or Dom Bruno (1903–1981), directed a large rescue operation and personally made connections that protected several hundred Jews, mainly children, after the German occupation of Belgium. Initially, working from a monastery in Louvain near Brussels with the Comité de Défense des Juifs (Jewish Defense Committee), this Belgian Benedictine monk personally found shelter for children in religious and secular institutions and in private homes. Pedaling his bicycle across Belgium, he provided children with false identity and food ration cards and compensated host families. As he expanded the scope of his activities, he moved from place to place to avoid being caught. In January 1944 the Gestapo raided his monastery, and Father Bruno was forced into hiding. In disguise, out of his priest's habit, he continued to direct the rescue operation until Belgium's liberation in September 1944.

After liberation he walked into a synagogue in Brussels to see many of the children who had been reunited with their families. The rabbi proclaimed, "We have amongst us a hero, a hero who has devoted his life to save many of our children" (Singer, Testimony, *First Person* series). In 1964 he was recognized as one of the Righteous Among the Nations at Yad Vashem, and at the ceremony he remembered those who had opened their doors to the Jews. A tree was planted in his honor at Yad Vashem on May 21, 1991, and a memorial was constructed in Ottignies, Belgium, where he spent the last years of his life. He is also listed as a rescuer from Belgium on the Rescuers' Wall at the United States Holocaust Memorial Museum.

Jack Goldstein, Rachelle Silberman, and Flora Mendelowicz were among the children Father Bruno rescued. From an Orthodox family who had fled Vienna for Belgium, Jack recalled praying at a Belgian convent at the age of nine. Rachelle was just three when Father Bruno hid her. Jack and Rachelle met in the United States in 1955 and discovered that this same Belgian monk had saved them both. They later married.

Flora Mendelowicz Singer was a child when her parents left Romania in the 1920s for the safety of Antwerp, Belgium. When war broke out, they moved to Brussels. "I don't remember being a child," she confessed. She credits Father Bruno with saving her life; he was a saint to her and to many others (Singer, Testimony, *First Person* series). For her whole life, she remained grateful to him and to the sisters of Our Lady of Seven Sorrows. She stayed in touch with all of them.

Flora Mendelowicz in Belgium

Flora Mendelowicz Singer

Flora became a beloved teacher and later a volunteer at the United States Holocaust Memorial Museum, where she was my docent on one of my visits. Tenderly pointing to Father Bruno's name on the Rescuers' Wall, she described him as a saint and an angel who had saved her life, and leaning forward, she kissed the wall.

The Likeness of a Man

Swedish businessman turned diplomat Raoul Wallenberg (born in 1912, taken into Soviet custody in 1945, reported to have died in 1947) helped save the lives of tens of thousands of Hungarian Jews from the summer of 1944 to early 1945. Growing up fatherless in an aristocratic Swedish banking family, Raoul Wallenberg was guided by his paternal grandfather, who carefully mapped out broad educational and foreign experiences for his grandson and trained him from an early age to be a citizen of the world. He studied architecture at the University of Michigan and worked in financial institutions in South Africa and in Haifa after graduation. Wallenberg first encountered Jews fleeing from Nazi persecution while working for the Holland Bank in Haifa in 1936.

After the death of his grandfather, Wallenberg returned to Sweden, working as an executive of an import-export business that was headed by a Hungarian Jew. Through this commercial enterprise Wallenberg gained some knowledge of central Europe but was somewhat restless in following a career path in the initial years of the war. His awareness of the plight of the Jews would lend a focus to his abilities and skills.

With the support of the newly established American War Refugee Board and the World Jewish Congress, the Swedish Foreign Ministry selected Wallenberg to lead the War Refugee Board in its mission to help save the remaining two hundred thousand Jews of Budapest. He arrived in Budapest on July 9, 1944, and took many bold steps to achieve this goal. Working in concert with other diplomats, especially the like-minded Swiss consul to Budapest, Carl Lutz, Wallenberg and his staff created and handed out an official-looking passport, the *Schutzpass*, with the Swedish seal showing that the Swedish government protected the bearer. He jumped on trains headed for deadly destinations, demanding that those with protective documents be taken off the train. With his staff he used other documents to bring more Jews under his protective web, and he negotiated and bribed whenever he could to forestall deportations. He provided safe houses, nurseries, hospitals, and soup kitchens for Budapest's Jews. He seemed to be everywhere, and his mere presence lifted morale.

After the Soviet liberation/occupation of Budapest, Soviet agents detained Raoul Wallenberg on January 17, 1945. He was not heard from again. He was thirty-three years old when he disappeared.

In honor of his tremendous humanitarian work the United States Holocaust Memorial Museum named the street on which it is situated Raoul Wallenberg Place. His role as a rescuer is featured prominently at this museum. Yad Vashem named him one of the Righteous Among the Nations in 1963.

Raoul Wallenberg

NORWAY
SWEDEN
Scotland
NORTH SEA
Northern Ireland
UNITED KINGDOM
DENMARK
IRELAND
Wales
England
Berlin
NETHERLANDS
Bruges
Antwerp
Maaseik
GERMANY
ENGLISH CHANNEL
Brussels
Ottignies
Cologne
BELGIUM
LUX.
CZECH REPUBLIC
Vienna
FRANCE
AUSTRIA
SWITZERLAND
SLOVENIA
CROATIA
ADRIATIC SEA
ITALY
SPAIN
MEDITERRANEAN SEA

FINLAND

ESTONIA

LATVIA

Moscow

RUSSIA

BALTIC
SEA

LITHUANIA

Kovno

RUSSIA
Königsberg

BELARUS

POLAND

UKRAINE

SLOVAKIA

MOLDOVA

Budapest

HUNGARY

ROMANIA

BOSNIA
AND
HERZ.

SERBIA

BLACK SEA

MONT.

KOSOVO

BULGARIA

MACEDONIA

ALBANIA

GREECE

TURKEY

AEGEAN
SEA

Roundups

Roman Kniker at the villa garden before the war

Uprooted

For Roman Kent

Kilometers from Łódź,
we summer at our villa,
chasing soccer and volleyballs,
tasting fruits from Father's garden.
September war halts our play—
we leave behind ripe kernels,
swells of radish and roots,
the flavor of strawberrysweet days.

In Marysin,
the better part of Ghetto Łódź,
Brother and I turn stones to till our plot.
Some cede their patch to Father for cash;
our ground grows by squares.
Cabbage, lettuce, cucumbers give life.
Potatoes sprout from buried eyes.
Beets, carrots, and radishes seed
dreams beyond the leather factory
where we sew knapsacks for the enemy.
We stand guard over our crops.

Roundups send the last of Łódź to trains.
Before they leave, the leaving
pick our every ear and leaf and stem,
the nightshades that foreshadow hunger.
I sob over wasted work,
though buried potatoes still feed
until we, too, are found.

After Auschwitz and Flossenbürg,
Brother and I sail for New York—
orphans.

Bureaus send us south to a dot of map
that I know from *Gone with the Wind*:
red clay glazed in fire,
planted rows strewn with leathered
harnesses and hoof prints,
hunger.
Their restored homes and gardens
sit grand and green.
We stand alone in a house of strangers,
our story driven underground
like potatoes in Łódź.

Roman at the garden in Marysin, Łódź Ghetto, August 1944

Roman at his first home in Atlanta, 1946

Feathers

gossip, like feathers,
ripped, scattered from pillows, ill
will blows to earth's end

night of shattered glass,
bedding feathers fill courtyards,
fears couch worried heads

ghettoed Jews to trains,
swirls of feather clouds remain,
wave the lone farewell

"birds of a feather"?
some say nazis had no choice,
flock with no free will

"birds of a feather"—
what an insult to birds who
kill only to eat

The Witness Stands

The trees look ominous, like judges.
   —YEVGENY YEVTUSHENKO, "Babi Yar"

Majestic trees,
pairs of eyes, east and west,
watch what happens here

Linden in Berlin,
fragrant blossoms, heart-shaped leaves—
no love lost on Jews

White birch of Kiev,
petrified of uniforms,
blinded by bullets

Warsaw Ghetto's trees,
felled by Nazi policy,
carved names turn to dust

Poplars in Auschwitz,
frightened by flames, man's
painful forced parade

Birkenau's birch groves
tremble as chamber music
dances down Alma's bow

Sobibór's sentinels
see prisoners past the minefields,
silencing the gas

Clusters of firs,
White Russian woods hide
partisan retreats

Pine needles point:
"Bielski's Partisans Were Here"—
betrayers beware

Bielskis on the run
perch in treetop beds by night,
eyes on enemies

Tall trees sliced in half,
laid across the railroad tracks,
steel undone by wood

Anne's white horse chestnut
hosts wings, branches glisten,
court signs of spring

Rooted in the earth,
listening, recording truth
buried in their rings.

Memories in Color

The secret agent
marks the San Fernando map with colored lines:
house on Garibaldi with black X,
path to bus stop in broken blue,
bus route in forest green,
nearby streets as veins of red.
That night,
black and blue, red and green lines,
electrified as thunderbolts,
drown his heartbeats and nearly his words,
"*Un momentito, Señor.*"*
The agent's fur-lined gloves
(no bare hands over Señor's mouth)
grab and wrestle
the bony bus rider with polished shoes
into the waiting car.

At night,
marooned with the prisoner, the agent
marks over the *The South American Handbook* maps
(an accidental canvas) with
brown-penciled sketches of the captive.
Contours of his features
fall across Argentina:
staring, spectacled eyes,
bloodless lips
that barely say,
"*Ich bin Adolf Eichmann.*"*

By day,
the captor seeks solace in churches,
renewed by melodies, candles, icons,
quiet.

By evening,
he slips into songs and dances of Carnaval,
but in small hours of night
with eyes closed,
only darkness and dead family
frame long nights.
He paints lost sister and her three children
in Rouault's reds and leaden blacks,
reminders of the day when
"All that was delightful in the world died with them."†
He keeps them alive with his paintbrush:
"Memories that are blended in colors
are like flowers growing in the desert,
lonely but not forgotten . . ."‡

Reluctant portraits
of prisoner plant ideas:
haircut, lenses, lips, shoes
can change the captive.
"With the right mask, even Satan
can disguise himself as a human being"†—
or as an El Al steward
on his way back to Israel,
anesthetized for historic flight
to justice.

*Peter Malkin and Harry Stein, *Eichmann in My Hands.*
†Peter Malkin, *The Argentina Journal.*
‡Peter Malkin, inscribing my copy of *The Argentina Journal.*

Peter Malkin

Father Patrick Desbois

Misericordia for the Last Jews of Busk, Ukraine

For Father Patrick Desbois

Outside the cemetery one kid stood,
just one kid, only one kid,
with other goats, two horses, geese
past the ancient burial grid,

beyond the leafy little town
'round the river, bucolic scene,
until the Nazis swept through Busk,
drafting locals for tasks obscene:

Jewish men to dig the pits,
peasant men to bring a spade,
Jewish families shot en masse,
Ukrainian children watched and bade

their classmates, friends, a hushed good-bye.
From ruined time, they carried those
parting words of the Jews of Busk—
"Farewell, life"—the last words froze.

———————————

Atop a tombstone one kid poses,
just one goat, only one goat,
as a French priest and forensic team
photograph, record, take note

of wedding bands flung to the dirt,
capture words of those who saw
the rows of faces fall in place;
though time has passed, the scene is raw,

fresh-engraved on children's souls,
their fathers forced to bring a cart
to hasty grave for Jews they knew,
themselves assigned to take a part.

Words, long buried, finally spill,
unearthed in a hundred holes of fear
where Jews of Busk were butchered then
in ways that melt the eyes to tear.

Father Desbois extracts the facts,
invites the truth to surface now—
to count the lives, to mark the deaths
with *Kaddish* and his reverent bow.

misericordia: compassion, mercy (Latin).
Kaddish: Jewish memorial prayer (Aramaic).

Lost and *Found*

Roman and Lala

Uprooted

Roman Kent (Roman Kniker) was born in 1929 in Łódź, Poland, the son of Sonia and Emanuel Kniker, the owner of a textile factory in this industrial city. With two older sisters and Leon, his younger brother, he led a comfortable life with his family. Roman attended a Jewish school and enjoyed sports. In the summers, the family vacationed at their rural villa near Łódź, where they could bicycle, play ball, and have fun with their small golden-haired dog, Lala (Polish word for doll). Father ran the factory during the week and joined the family on weekends, when he enjoyed working in his abundant vegetable garden. This charmed life ended the moment war began.

Restrictions began for Jews with the defeat of Poland by the Germans in September 1939. Roman's family first relocated to a room in his father's factory, and in March 1940 they moved to the Łódź Ghetto. Living quarters were tight, and activities and food supplies were severely restricted. Surprisingly, Lala made her own journey to the ghetto to reunite with them, dividing her time between the human family and her litter. Shortly thereafter, the Germans ordered that all dogs must be turned over to them.

An order of May 1940 by the Department of Gardens and Land Cultivation, which was under the *Judenrat* headed by Mordechai Chaim Rumkowski, allowed families to use a plot of land for gardening. The tillers were permitted to keep their yield, providing essential food (YIVO Institute for Jewish Research). Roman's father purchased additional plots from Jews who were not able to farm the land. At this time Roman and Leon worked with other young people in the Leder and Sattler Ressort leather factory sewing knapsacks, belts, and all types of goods for the German army, but they also tended the garden. They cleared stony soil with shovels to plant cabbage, cauliflower, tomatoes, lettuce, carrots, beets, cucumbers, and radishes; potatoes were planted whole. In November 1942 their malnourished father became acutely ill with ulcers and died shortly after.

Roman and other Jewish boys of the Łódź Ghetto at the Leder and Sattler Ressort factory

The boys shouldered the responsibility of feeding the family—raking, planting, watering, weeding, and fretting over their crops.

At summer's end in 1944, Jews were grabbed and dragged to the trains. On their way the deportees raided food supplies. Roman armed himself with sticks and brooms, but the Kniker family garden was ravished by the famished Jews: "I stood in the middle of the field with my head bowed, unable to stop sobbing" (Kent, *Courage Was My Only Option*). His family, too, was deported soon after and sent to Auschwitz, where his mother was murdered.

Roman and Leon were sent on to other camps. On April 23, 1945, while marching from Flossenbürg to Dachau, they were liberated by American soldiers of Patton's Third Army. Because President Truman issued a directive that loosened restrictions on immigrants displaced by the Nazi regime, the brothers came to New York in 1946 and were placed with a prosperous Jewish family in Atlanta, a city only known to Roman from his prewar reading of *Gone with the Wind* in Polish. This first host family seemed emotionally detached from the boys and neglected their nutritional needs. Roman protested, and the boys were moved to a more nurturing home and flourished. Roman was the first to attend Emory University, and Leon followed. Roman made his career in international trade in New York, and Leon became a neurosurgeon.

Roman has dedicated himself to Holocaust education. He shares his story through his autobiography, *Courage Was My Only Option*, and in *My Dog Lala* for younger readers. He has played a leadership role in nearly every major Holocaust organization: the Jewish Foundation for the Righteous, the American Gathering of Jewish Holocaust Survivors, the Conference on Jewish Material Claims Against Germany, the American Friends of Tel Aviv University, and the United States Holocaust Memorial Council. His wife, Hannah, herself a Holocaust survivor who was raised and educated in Łódź, has been a tremendous support for him in his legendary work. I met this gracious, kind man and his lovely wife at a joint American Gathering/Holocaust educators' conference in Washington, DC.

Roman and Hannah Kent

Feathers

A Jewish folk story tells of a woman who suspects that she has caused damage by spreading tales about another villager. She talks with her rabbi, who counsels her to slit a down pillow and watch the feathers scatter; her task will be to retrieve the feathers and place them back into the pillowcase. She objects that she cannot gather all the feathers, and the rabbi says that the same is true of gossip: it cannot be returned to its source. Similarly, the Nazis stirred up negative feelings towards Jews by spreading lies about them. Many of these lies circulated throughout Germany in the 1930s.

On November 9 and 10, 1938, also known as *Kristallnacht*, glass shards were flying in the night. In Germany and Austria, hundreds of synagogues were set on fire, and glass storefronts of more than seven thousand Jewish businesses were broken, trashed, and looted. Jewish hospitals, cemeteries, and homes were plundered. More than ninety Jews were killed on that night, and thirty thousand were arrested and sent to Buchenwald, Dachau, and Sachsenhausen, all concentration camps in Germany. Many Jews died in the month that followed as a result of these events. What many women recalled of that night, though, were feathers flying as they looked on, their homes torn apart, their men taken away.

From the ghettos in Poland, Nazis rounded up Jews in a brutal way and sent them toward deadly destinations. In searching their homes, Nazi soldiers often slashed feather pillows and blankets, checking to see that no persons or valuables were left behind. Ben Helfgott (b. 1929) reports that from October 14 to 21, 1942, about twenty-two thousand of the twenty-four thousand Jews in the ghetto in Piotrków Trybunalski, Poland, were deported to the gas chambers of Treblinka. Because he was working at a glass factory in a labor camp outside of the ghetto, Ben was spared at age twelve. He remembers returning to the ghetto to find a dense cloud of floating feathers tumbling over his neighborhood where friends and family had lived hours before (Epstein).

On November 28, 1944, Ben and his father were taken from the ghetto to Buchenwald concentration camp, and a week later Ben was transferred to another camp. He never saw his father again. Ben was sent to several camps, including Schlieben, Buchenwald, and Theresienstadt. In May 1945 he left Theresienstadt weighing eighty pounds.

In August 1945 Ben Helfgott was permitted to come to Great Britain on a program sponsored by the British government and the Jewish philanthropist Leonard Montefiore. One thousand children who survived and did not have family to care for them were eligible to enter Great Britain under this program, but only 732 could be found. In Britain he thrived in this group of child survivors known as "The Boys," eventually learning to speak nine languages.

In 1948, while still living with other Boys in a transition house in London, Ben observed a group of men lifting weights. Impulsively, he joined them, surprising their coach with his skill. He began weightlifting that year and by 1956 was able to represent

Great Britain as a weightlifter in the Olympics. He served as team captain of the 1956 and 1960 Olympic teams.

Since 1963 Ben Helfgott has served as chairman of a charitable organization whose members were originally all Boys but that now also includes the Boys' family members. Since his youth he has been inspired to do good in the world by the example and books of Dr. Janusz Korczak, the doctor of the Warsaw orphanage ("His Overtures of Love").

Ben Helfgott at the World Weightlifting Championship in Warsaw, 1959

The Witness Stands

What if the trees could reveal what they had seen? What history did they witness?

The Jews of Germany were progressively segregated from public places, including parks, restaurants, swimming pools, and movie theaters. Specially marked park benches were often designated for Jews. Many of these same restrictions were imposed in other European countries after the German armed forces invaded. Flora Singer ("Kissing the Wall"), for example, living in Antwerp, Belgium, reported sadness and anger when she and her sisters could not visit their favorite neighborhood public park (Singer, Testimony, *First Person* series).

Jews who were ordered into the Warsaw Ghetto were deprived of proper nutrition, health care, sanitation, living quarters, even the beauty of trees. Chaim Kaplan recorded in his diary on June 17, 1942: "We have been robbed of every tree and every flower."

The east turned deadly for Jews. Birch trees stood near sites of mass murder by the *Einsatzgruppen*: near Kiev, for example, 33,771 Jews were murdered at the ravine Babi Yar in September 1941. When the killing shifted to the death camps in German-occupied Poland, poplars in Auschwitz stood in the shadows of the forced parade of inmates lining up at roll call twice a day and at the will of the Nazis. Alma Rosé and the women in the orchestra she conducted at Auschwitz-Birkenau played music as the slave laborers marched to and from work. Nearly all of these musicians survived because they played in this orchestra. The word *"Birkenau"* means "birch groves" in German.

When the true destinations of trains rolling out of the ghettos became known, some Jews attempted to run for the nearby forests. Amidst the fir trees of the Belorussian woods, some sought shelter. Here different types of partisan camps emerged. Family camps hid Jews who had fled from ghettos and other locations and provided sanctuary and support. Their main goal was to keep Jews alive. After the murder of their parents and two brothers in

December 1941, the Bielski brothers—Tuvia, Zus, and Asael—headed this type of camp in the Naliboki Forest.

One division of the Bielski outfit did, however, fight with weapons, and this branch exemplifies another variety of partisan camp, the military unit whose goal was to battle the enemy with arms and diversionary tactics. Armed partisans derailed German trains by placing felled trees on the tracks and using mines to ignite the trains. They destroyed supplies for the enemy and headed off attacks on the family camps. They, like the partisan Leibke Kaganowicz ("*Patzan*"), felt they had inflicted a significant strike against the Nazi war machine.

Bielski partisans . . .

The Bielski camp encountered opposition from some villagers and from the Germans. Villagers who betrayed them were punished so that the Jews would stand a chance to survive in the forest. Betrayers were identified and sometimes killed to discourage duplicity. The Bielskis were also hunted by the Germans in a concerted effort to destroy the partisan movement in August 1943. Tuvia Bielski's memoir, published in Israel in 1954, described this "big hunt" when members of the Bielski camp slept tied to tree trunks and atop the trees (Mais). More than twelve hundred Jews survived in the Bielski camp.

. . . and the family camp

Another response to the killing of Jews was rebellion at some of the death camps in German-occupied Poland. On October 14, 1943, one such rebellion broke out at Sobibór following a plan developed by the camp underground leader Leon Feldhendler and by Alexander Pechersky, a Soviet-Jewish prisoner of war who had recently arrived at Sobibór. After many SS and Ukrainian guards were killed and the camp was set on fire, the underground urged the permanent prisoners to run. Pechersky later recounted how escapees used trees for cover and for construction of a makeshift bridge (Mais). Soon after the uprising, the Germans destroyed the gas chambers, fences, and barracks at the death camp.

In 1944 Anne Frank gazed through a closed window of the Amsterdam attic at the white horse chestnut tree in the courtyard below, one of the few pleasures she was still able to enjoy.

Memories in Color

On May 11, 1960, in Buenos Aires, Argentina, one of the most infamous Nazis was captured by an Israeli Mossad team. Peter Zvi Malkin (1927–2005) was the secret agent on the team who seized Adolf Eichmann and wrestled the former Nazi officer into a waiting car as part of a daring plot to return him to Israel to be put on trial as a war criminal. The team identified, captured, interrogated, and sequestered Eichmann, the SS official in charge of deportation of the Jews, and then developed a plan to take him to Israel to stand trial for his crimes.

After the capture, agent Peter Malkin, who was also a gifted artist, took his turn guarding the prisoner. He began drawing the prisoner with sketching pencils, acrylic paints, and makeup he carried in his disguise kit. His canvas was a South American travel guide, and his images of Eichmann, his own family, churches, and Carnaval were superimposed on the pages of maps and text. His images and notes later became *The Argentina Journal.*

As an artist, Peter Malkin was the team member responsible for creating a disguise for Eichmann so that the prisoner could be secreted aboard an Israeli airliner that would take him from Argentina to Israel. Some of his sketches in the travel guide constituted a study of Eichmann's features and demeanor, a study necessary to create a convincing transformation. Malkin's suggestions of changing the prisoner's hairstyle, lip shape, and shoes were used to dress Eichmann as an ailing El Al steward. On May 21, 1960, the El Al airplane that transported the unrecognizable Eichmann and some of the Mossad agents cleared Argentina's airspace en route to Israel.

In Israel, Eichmann was tried behind bulletproof glass in a closely observed courtroom from April 11 through August 14, 1961. He was charged with crimes against the Jewish people and against humanity and for war crimes.

Peter Malkin of Israel, after a portrait by Malkin
on a map of Argentina in The South American Handbook

Eichmann was found guilty and was sentenced to die in December. He was executed in Israel on May 31, 1962.

Peter Malkin spent twenty-seven years in the Mossad, and he retired as chief of operations in 1976. After retirement he worked as an artist, author, lecturer, and consultant on international antiterrorism efforts.

Shortly after the release of *The Argentina Journal*, I met Peter Malkin. The editor of the *Journal* brought him to my home for a brief visit. He was a strong, confident man who was very articulate and gentle in manner. He commented about the Argentina experience: "I never carried a gun; my brain was my weapon." Everything I had learned about him from his books and from our meeting seemed to confirm his self-assessment.

Misericordia for the Last Jews of Busk, Ukraine

After the German invasion of the Soviet Union in June 1941, the Nazis took their campaign to Ukraine, Belorussia, Russia, eastern Poland, and Moldavia, murdering between 1.25 and 1.5 million Jews. Babi Yar, near Kiev, Ukraine, is the most well-known site of the murders by the *Einsatzgruppen*, the mobile killing squads. Father Patrick Desbois, a Catholic priest from France, reported in 2015 that he had uncovered more than seventeen hundred similar sites in a quest of his own to document this "Holocaust by Bullets."

Although a broad brush paints this terrible chapter, the history of each village is distinct. In Busk, a village in western Ukraine, Jews had lived for centuries. Their first synagogue, built in 1502, and a magnificent ancient cemetery still stood at the time of the German invasion. The Wehrmacht took possession of Busk on July 1, 1941, just days after Germany had invaded the Soviet Union. On Yom Kippur, September 1942, approximately seven hundred Jews of Busk were killed in the first *Aktion* against them, and the surviving Jews were forced into a ghetto two months later. On May 21, 1943, the German Security Police, Ukrainian police, and some ethnic Germans living outside of Germany murdered more than twelve hundred Jews there. Several hundred Jews deemed fit to work were transferred to the Yanovska camp in Lvov.

Many Ukrainian children witnessed these killings and were forced to participate in some of the postexecution tasks. In Busk, those who were children at the time and who are now elders have testified about the roles their fathers, cousins, and neighbors played and of their own assignments at the scene of the crime. The memory of this time is still very vivid for them, and most witnesses seem relieved to tell what they had seen and done so long ago. Father Desbois and his team of ballistics experts, linguists, historians, and photographers urge these witnesses to give details about where and how the killings occurred. Before arriving at each village, Father Desbois and his team thoroughly research the history of each site using German and Soviet archives to be able to ask specific questions to document the history, often for the first time.

Father Desbois is the founder and president of Yahad–In Unum, Hebrew and Latin words that mean "together." Established in 2004, this organization of French Catholic and Jewish leaders facilitates communication between Catholics and Jews and provides a respectful, dignified memorial for those Jews killed in Ukraine. He acts in full accordance with Jewish customs and laws for honoring the dead and is grateful that finally a Jewish prayer is said in their memory. Under his direct leadership, the organization sponsors visits to sites where murders took place. His *The Holocaust by Bullets: A Priest's Journey to Uncover the Truth Behind the Murder of 1.5 Million Jews* documents his remarkable work.

The mining of memory by Father Desbois raises several questions: What is the price of keeping the secrets of what happened here? Does a memory of a good deed last longer than the memory of an evil deed, or vice versa? How does Father Desbois compare what he sees with what he does not see and has to piece together? What allows individuals such as Father Desbois to dedicate themselves to such difficult projects?

NORWAY
SWEDEN
Scotland
NORTH SEA
Northern Ireland
UNITED KINGDOM
DENMARK
IRELAND
Wales
England
Amsterdam
Sachsenhausen
London
NETHERLANDS
Berlin
Antwerp
Schlieben
ENGLISH CHANNEL
BELGIUM
Buchenwald
GERMANY
Terezin/ Theresienstadt
LUX.
Flossenbürg
CZECH REPUBLIC
Dachau
FRANCE
SWITZERLAND
AUSTRIA
SLOVENIA
CROATIA
ADRIATIC SEA
ITALY
SPAIN
MEDITERRANEAN SEA

* Showing present-day borders

FINLAND

ESTONIA

LATVIA

BALTIC
SEA

LITHUANIA

RUSSIA

RUSSIA

Naliboki
Forest

BELARUS

POLAND

Treblinka

Łódź

Warsaw

Sobibór

Piotrków
Trybunalski

Auschwitz

Busk

Lvov

Kiev

UKRAINE

SLOVAKIA

MOLDOVA

HUNGARY

ROMANIA

BLACK SEA

BOSNIA
AND
HERZ.

SERBIA

MONT.

KOSOVO

MACEDONIA

BULGARIA

ALBANIA

GREECE

AEGEAN
SEA

TURKEY

Close Connections

Smuggling through the wall of the Warsaw Ghetto

Recounting

Parents, locked in Warsaw's cage
when rage of black boots clattered,
tried to tend their girls and boys—
those who truly mattered.

Mothers told the truth to them,
why food supplies ran dry,
that mothers had no appetite
(sons knew this was a lie).

Crawling through the cracks of wall,
boys smuggled at age six,
breadwinners for the families,
dinner through the bricks.

Parents feared their famished girls
whose waists were growing small
would never dream a wedding gown,
now shrouded in a shawl.

As Jews here in America,
we dread what we must tell
to our own children, innocent—
we serve a slice of hell.

We say it couldn't happen here
or start up once again;
we guard our words and gauge our tone
to pray it's true. Amen.

Anne Frank and Petr Ginz

Close Connections: 1938–1946

Emanuel Ringelblum for the Joint
leaves for Zbąszyń, helping those
dumped by Germans. Does he serve
Grynszpan's family as they compose

the plaintive post that ignites their son
Herschel in Paris, who in fright and rage
shoots vom Rath, whose death inspires
flames from well-rehearsèd stage?

Escorting *Kinder* on the train
to Britain from the German towns,
Norbert hosts a sea of youth—
perhaps Fritz Westfeld?—on his rounds.

In Ghetto Łódź Chava Rosenfarb
at seventeen, the youngest chair
in Miriam Ulinover's home,
shares Yiddish lyrics in the lair.

Pavel Friedmann and Anne Frank
report their worlds though worlds apart.
He misses yellow butterflies;
her shuttered hours she starts to chart.

Vladka nears Dr. Ringelblum's desk,
requesting cards to show they're working—
her mother, brother, and herself—
buying time with death trains lurking.

Dr. Korczak in Warsaw, tending his orphans,
stretches his hand to temper their fears.
Beneath white stars, Sutzkever in Vilna
seeks heaven's vise to cradle his tears.

The Karmel sisters and mother labor
at Skarżysko-Kamienna, Poland, as slaves,
and stand for roll call—near Chanka and sisters?
Can Chanka hear Henia's orations and raves?

Welding at Auschwitz, Norbert Wollheim
may hear a phrase of Schubert or Bach.
From Alma's baton Beethoven beckons
as newcomers first find comfort, then shock.

Pavel and Petr, plucked from Terezin,
poets of promise guaranteed to be caught,
are cast to die in the ashes of Auschwitz,
youth gifted with words carefully wrought.

In only a heartbeat young people of letters,
poems, and stories are captured midair—
Pavel, Petr, and Anne Frank at Auschwitz
pass through the gates, no manuscripts there.

Chanka and sisters are trapped in the same camp
where typhus takes Margot and Annelies Frank.
For those who still breathe, the marching continues
for Norbert, for Chanka, Karmels at the flank.

When Wallenberg's forced to a Soviet prison
or torturous site they will never reveal,
perhaps he sees Sugihara in passing—
both rescued their thousands by stamping a seal.

Eighty pounds, Ben Helfgott leaves Terezin
in May '45 as the hellish war ends,
arriving too late to meet Petr and Pavel,
tenacious fighters who might have been friends.

Nesa, a bride of Mother's invention,
parachutes into betrothed and behold.
Roman now lands in the red clay of Georgia,
rooted in soil, but his story untold.

Flora, a Singer, grateful to Father
Bruno of Belgium, kisses the wall.
Wise from Szydłowiec, Tess still remembers—
addressing the facts, teaching us all.

Dr. Janusz Korczak escorting his children,
Abraham Sutzkever charging his pen,
Chanka and Henia, Norbert and Fritz,
Vladka, Ilona, Wallenberg, Anne,
Sugihara, Ringelblum, Petr, and Pavel,
Miriam, Chava, Alma, and Ben.

Hannah Senesh as a teenager in Budapest

There are stars whose radiance is visible on earth long after they themselves are gone. There are people whose glorious memory continues to light the world though they are no longer among the living. These lights are particularly bright when the night is dark. They light the way.

—HANNAH SENESH, letter sent by Hannah to her mother's family in Dombóvár, Hungary, upon the death of her great-aunt Betti Mama, September 1940

An Unexpected Afterword

Michael Berenbaum, the profound and prolific scholar of the Holocaust, asks, "After the last survivor is no longer, who will remember, who will tell their stories?" Just as I was completing *Beneath White Stars*, Elie Wiesel died. This eloquent speaker and moral leader was not the last survivor, but his death made these questions even more poignant. I add my tribute to one who dedicated his life to teaching us to remember the Holocaust and to allow it to transform our character and our future.

Taking Sides

In memory of Elie Wiesel (1928-2016)

No gesture or ornament distracts us
as you speak,
though night vision dims
our view of ourselves.
You forbid
despair-breeding silence,
for silence still
serves the foe.
You call us to take sides
with the victim,
to stand in his place
in the center of the universe.

Only a fall of hair
and story lines folded into your face
soften steely words.
Sowing seeds,
you tell of things that hover in the air,
linking the tragedy of you and yours
with them and theirs
and us.

July 7, 2016

Timeline:
Key Events for People in the Poems

1933

- Miriam Ulinover continues to write poems in Łódź, Poland.
- The poet Gertrud Kolmar from Berlin writes "In the Camp" predicting horrors to come.
- Otto Frank and his family leave Frankfurt, Germany, for Amsterdam.
- More than 530 Jewish businesses close in Frankfurt this year.

1936

- The older brother of Fritz Westfeld (Fred Westfield) travels to Nashville, Tennessee, to live with family.

1938

• March 12–13	German troops invade Austria, unifying Austria and Germany. Adolf Eichmann and the SS intimidate Jews to encourage emigration from Austria.
• June	Anne Frank plays at Amstelrust Park, Amsterdam.
• July 6–15	Delegates to the Évian Conference discuss immigration options for the Jews of Germany.
• October 30	The Joint Distribution Committee sends Dr. Emanuel Ringelblum to Zbąszyń, Poland, to help Jews who were forcibly removed from Germany.
• November 9–10	*Kristallnacht.* Two weeks after this night of violence, Walter Westfeld, a prominent art dealer in Düsseldorf, Germany, and uncle of Fritz Westfeld (Fred Westfield), is arrested.
•	In the aftermath of *Kristallnacht* Norbert Wollheim helps to organize and administer the *Kindertransport* program.
• December 1	The first *Kindertransport* train leaves Germany for Great Britain.

1939

• January	Fritz Westfeld (Fred Westfield) boards a *Kindertransport* train in Essen, Germany, for London.
• March 15	The German army enters Czechoslovakia and occupies Prague. Anti-Jewish laws that affect the family of Petr Ginz and others will be in place four months later.
• May	More than half of the Jews of Frankfurt have left the city.
• May 13	The SS *St. Louis* with Jewish refugees aboard leaves Hamburg, Germany, for Havana, Cuba.
• May 17	The British government issues a White Paper restricting the number of Jews who can enter Palestine.
• June 6	Denied entry to Cuba, the SS *St. Louis* returns to Europe with most passengers still aboard.
• September 1	World War II begins as the German military forces invade Poland. Persecution of Poland's Jews begins immediately. The establishment of Jewish ghettos in German-occupied Poland will follow.
•	The last *Kindertransport* train departs from Berlin.
•	Operation Pied Piper relocates many British children and children from the *Kindertransport* to the countryside. Fritz Westfeld (Fred Westfield) is among them.
• Fall	Chiune Sugihara is sent to Kovno, Lithuania, as Japanese consul general.

1940

•	Miriam Ulinover hosts a writers' circle in the Łódź Ghetto until the spring of 1944.
• February	Frankfurt's Jews are forced to turn their apartments over to German authorities.
• March	The family of Roman Kniker (Kent) moves to the Łódź Ghetto.
• April 9	The German army invades Denmark and Norway.
• May	Nelly Sachs leaves Berlin for Sweden and writes about Germany's treatment of Jews.
• May 10	The German army invades the Netherlands and Belgium.

- May 11   Łódź Ghetto's Department of Gardens and Land Cultivation offers land to those who wish to grow vegetables, including the family of Roman Kniker (Kent).
- May 13   The German army crosses into France.
- June   The Soviet Union annexes Lithuania, which then ceases to be a haven for Polish Jews who have fled there.
- June 14   The German army occupies Paris.
- July 27   Chiune Sugihara finds hundreds of Jews seeking help at the gates of the Japanese consulate in Kovno. He starts writing visas for them.
- Fall   Fritz Westfeld (Fred Westfield) and his parents leave England for New York and settle in Nashville.
- November   With the establishment of the Warsaw Ghetto, Dr. Janusz Korczak moves his orphanage inside the ghetto walls.
- •   Dr. Emanuel Ringelblum forms the Oyneg Shabes organization in Warsaw.
- December   Rescue efforts begin at Le Chambon-sur-Lignon, France, and continue through September 1944.

1941

- •   Tousia Goldberg (Tess Wise) and her family move into the Radom Ghetto in Poland.
- March   Forced labor begins for some Frankfurt Jews.
- June 22   The German forces invade the Soviet Union. The *Einsatzgruppen* start killing Jews the next day.
- June 24   The German army invades Vilna, Lithuania.
- June 26   The German army invades Šiauliai, Lithuania. Several thousand Jews are murdered in the forest. The family of Nesa Galperin (Nesse Godin) is sent to the ghetto.
- July   The *Einsatzgruppen* and Lithuanian collaborators begin killing most of Vilna's Jews at the Ponary Forest. The poet Abraham Sutzkever is sent to the Vilna Ghetto and will stay there until September 1943.
- July 1   German forces enter Busk, Ukraine.

• September 25–26	The *Einsatzgruppen* and Lithuanian collaborators murder most of the Jews of Eishyshok, Lithuania. Leibke Kaganowicz (Leon Kahn) witnesses the killings.
• September 29–30	The *Einsatzgruppen* murder 33,771 Jews at Babi Yar near Kiev, Ukraine.
• Fall	Jews in Frankfurt are deported to ghettos in Łódź, Kovno, and Minsk (Belorussia).
• December	In Czechoslovakia, the deportation of Prague's Jews to Terezin begins.
• December 7	Parents and two siblings of Tuvia, Asael, and Zus Bielski are murdered in Novogrudok, Belorussia. The Bielski brothers start amassing weapons.
• December 8	In the Łódź Ghetto, Mordechai Chaim Rumkowski prohibits Mendel Grossman from taking photographs for "private purposes." Grossman continues to take photographs secretly.

1942

•	Jews of Frankfurt are deported to Majdanek and Sobibór in Poland and to Terezin.
• Spring	Tousia Goldberg (Tess Wise) escapes from the labor camp in the Radom Ghetto. She will make her way to a town near Lublin, Poland, where she will stay until the fall of 1944 when the Red Army liberates the area.
• April 26	Pavel Friedmann of Prague is deported to Terezin.
• May 10	The *Einsatzgruppen* and collaborators murder most of the Jews of Radun, near Eishyshok, hometown of Leibke Kaganowicz (Leon Kahn).
• June 4	Pavel Friedmann's "The Butterfly" from Terezin bears this date.
• June 14	Anne Frank starts writing in her diary.
• June 17	From the Warsaw Ghetto, the diarist Chaim Kaplan writes: "We have been robbed of every tree and every flower."
• July	The poet Trude Groag is sent to Terezin, where she works as a teacher and a nurse.
• July 6	Anne Frank's family goes into hiding in Amsterdam.
• July 16	Paris policemen start rounding up 13,152 Jews.

- July 22   Deportations to Treblinka, Poland, begin in the Warsaw Ghetto. Feigele Peltel (Vladka Meed) hopes that employment cards will spare her family.
- August 3   As conditions worsen in the Warsaw Ghetto, the first part of the Oyneg Shabes Archive is buried.
- August 5   The Nazis round up Dr. Janusz Korczak and the children in his Warsaw orphanage for deportation to Treblinka.
- Fall   Feigele Peltel (Vladka Meed) joins the Jewish Coordinating Committee to help the Jewish Fighting Organization in the Warsaw Ghetto.
- September 21   The first *Aktion* is carried out against the Jews of Busk, Ukraine.
- October   Chanka Garfinkel (Helen Greenspun) and two siblings are taken from their hometown, Chmielnik, Poland, to the Skarżysko-Kamienna labor camp in Poland.
- October 14–21   Most of the Jews of the Piotrków Trybunalski Ghetto, Poland, where Ben Helfgott's family is living, are deported to Treblinka.
- October 22   Petr Ginz is deported from Prague to Terezin.
- November   A ghetto is set up for the remaining Jews in Busk.
- •   Vladka (later Meed), as Feigele Peltel is now nicknamed, is smuggled out of the Warsaw Ghetto to be a courier on the Aryan side, purchasing arms on the black market.
- December 18   From Terezin, Petr Ginz writes for and edits *Vedem*. The first issue appears on this date.

1943

- January   Father Bruno (Henri Reynders) starts rescuing Jews, mainly children, in Belgium.
- •   Leibke Kaganowicz (Leon Kahn) narrowly evades deportation from Grodno, Belorussia, and will soon join the Russian partisans.
- February   Dr. Emanuel Ringelblum orders the burial of the second part of the Oyneg Shabes Archive in milk cans.

- March   The poets Ilona and Henia Karmel work at the slave labor camp in Płaszów near their hometown, Kraków, Poland. They and their mother will be sent to Skarżysko-Kamienna, where the sisters will continue to write poems.
- March 2   The poet Gertrud Kolmar is deported to Auschwitz and dies soon after her arrival.
- March 11   From Berlin, Norbert Wollheim and his family are deported to Auschwitz.
- April 19   The Warsaw Ghetto Uprising begins and continues for more than three weeks.
- May 19–21   The ghetto in Busk is liquidated by mass shootings.
- June   Norbert Wollheim works as a welder at the I. G. Farben factory at Buna/Monowitz, Auschwitz.
- July   The violinist Alma Rosé is transported from Drancy, France, to Auschwitz-Birkenau and is soon selected to lead the women's orchestra.
- August   Dr. Emanuel Ringelblum is brought to Warsaw. While hiding in a bunker with his family, he writes his treatise on Polish-Jewish relations.
- August 1   The "big hunt" begins as German forces search to kill partisans, including the Bielskis, in the Naliboki Forest in western Belorussia.
- September   German soldiers hunt the forest where Abraham Sutzkever hides after the failed uprising in the Vilna Ghetto.
- October   Petr Ginz records his "Plans" and "Reports" at Terezin.
- October 1–2   The Danes rescue twelve hundred Jews by ferrying them to Sweden.
- October 14   Leon Feldhendler and Sasha Pechersky lead the revolt at Sobibór.

1944

- January   The Gestapo raids Father Bruno Reynders's monastery in Belgium, but he continues to rescue Jewish children.
- January 26   The War Refugee Board is established.

- **February** — Adolf Eichmann visits Auschwitz-Birkenau to discuss the arrangements for the arrival of 500,000 Hungarian Jews scheduled for deportation. He hears the women's orchestra perform under the direction of Alma Rosé.
- **February 23** — Anne Frank first writes in her diary about the horse chestnut tree in the courtyard.
- **March** — The poet Hannah Senesh parachutes into Yugoslavia as a British agent and emissary to help Jews in her native Hungary.
- **March 7** — Dr. Emanuel Ringelblum, his wife, and his son are betrayed. They are all murdered on March 10.
- **March 19** — German military forces occupy Hungary.
- **April 5** — Alma Rosé dies at Auschwitz of uncertain causes.
- **May** — Heinrich Himmler orders the liquidation of the Łódź Ghetto, the last remaining ghetto in Poland, with a population of approximately 75,000 Jews.
- **May 15** — Hungarian Jews in great numbers are deported to Auschwitz.
- **June** — Hannah Senesh crosses into Hungary and is soon captured, imprisoned, and tortured.
- **June 23** — Representatives from the International Red Cross and Danish Red Cross inspect Terezin. The camp has been "beautified" for their visit.
- **Summer** — Chanka Garfinkel (Helen Greenspun) and her siblings are shipped with other Skarżysko-Kamienna prisoners to Częstochowa, Poland.
- Henia and Ilona Karmel are sent to a forced labor factory attached to Buchenwald in central Germany. They sew their poems inside the hems of their dresses.
- **July** — When the Russian army liberates Vilna, Abraham Sutzkever and other partisans, including the poet Abba Kovner, recover Jewish books they had hidden.
- The Russian army liberates the area where the Bielski family camp is based. Bielski's Jews are ordered to leave the forest.

- The Šiauliai Ghetto in Lithuania is liquidated. Nesa Galperin (Nesse Godin) and her mother are sent to the Stutthof camp near the Baltic Sea. Nesa will be moved to four other labor camps.

- July 9 — Representing the War Refugee Board, Raoul Wallenberg arrives in Budapest, Hungary, to try to save the Jews from deportation.

- July 31 — The US Army Eighth Air Force B-24 bomber carrying Lead Crew #20 for the 389th Bombardment Group is shot down on a mission aiming to hit a methanol-processing building of I. G. Farben chemical works in Ludwigshafen, Germany. Surviving airmen are now prisoners of war. Herman Lodinger (lead bombardier and the author's father) is soon sent to Stalag Luft III, a camp for Air Force officers, in Sagan, Germany.

- August — More than 68,000 people from the Łódź Ghetto are sent to Auschwitz-Birkenau, including the poets Miriam Ulinover and Chava Rosenfarb. Miriam is murdered there; Chava will soon be sent on to camps in Germany, including Bergen-Belsen.

- August 4 — Anne Frank's family is arrested in Amsterdam. Her diary is left behind. On August 8 the family is sent to Westerbork, a transit camp in the Netherlands.

- September 3 — Anne Frank and her family are sent to Auschwitz.

- September 28 — Petr Ginz is deported from Terezin to Auschwitz. He perishes there. A boy remaining at their barrack in Terezin buries eight hundred pages of *Vedem*.

- September 29 — Pavel Friedmann, deported from Terezin, dies in Auschwitz.

- October 28 — Anne Frank and her sister, Margot, are sent to Bergen-Belsen.

- November — Adolf Eichmann organizes forced marches in Budapest. Raoul Wallenberg issues thousands of protective documents, chases convoys carrying Jews, and demands that German and Hungarian officers release Jews in their custody.

• November 7	The poet and parachutist Hannah Senesh is executed by a firing squad in Hungary.

1945

• January	Nesa Galperin (Nesse Godin) leaves Stutthof in north central Poland on a death march. The Russian army liberates her in March.
•	Chanka Garfinkel (Helen Greenspun) and her sisters are forced on a train to Bergen-Belsen.
• January 17	Soviet officials arrest Raoul Wallenberg.
• January 18	Auschwitz is evacuated. Norbert Wollheim is sent on a death march and is then crowded onto a train.
• January 27	All prisoners of war at Stalag Luft III are sent on foot out of the camp in blizzard conditions. Herman Lodinger is among them.
• March	Anne Frank and her sister die from typhus in Bergen-Belsen.
• March 5	From Bergen-Belsen, Chanka Garfinkel (Helen Greenspun) and her sisters are taken to other German camps: Burgau, Türkheim, Dachau, and Allach.
• April	The Karmel sisters and their mother are forced on a death march from Buchenwald. Henia's husband locates the sisters in September in Leipzig, Germany. They are taken to Sweden for surgeries.
• April 15	The British reach Bergen-Belsen. Chava Rosenfarb is suffering from typhus.
• April 20	From Sachsenhausen-Oranienburg, Germany, Norbert Wollheim and other camp inmates are marched out, guarded by the SS.
• April 23	While on a forced march from Flossenbürg to Dachau, Roman and Leon Kniker (Kent) are liberated by Patton's Third Army.
• April 29	Chanka Garfinkel (Helen Greenspun) and her sisters are liberated by American forces at Allach, a subcamp of Dachau. Chanka and sister Bela have typhus.

- American prisoners of war, now amassed at Moosburg in southeastern Germany, are liberated by Patton's Third Army. Herman Lodinger is among more than one hundred thousand prisoners of war assembled here. Later General Patton himself addresses the former prisoners.
- May Tousia Goldberg (Tess Wise) reunites with surviving family members and later moves to Germany, where she will attend medical school at the University of Munich.
- May 2 Norbert Wollheim flees to Schwerin, Germany, and is freed by American soldiers.
- May 9 Fifteen-year-old Ben Helfgott walks out of Terezin weighing eighty pounds.
- After the war The Sugihara family is imprisoned in a Soviet internment camp for eighteen months.
- Tuvia and Zus Bielski immigrate to Palestine, where they will fight in Israel's War of Independence.
- Summer Chanka Garfinkel (Helen Greenspun) lives at DP camps in Germany through 1949.
- Chava Rosenfarb crosses the border of Germany into Belgium, where she will live as a displaced person for several years.
- August Nesa (Nesse) Galperin marries Yankel (Jack) Godin. The newlyweds and Nesa's mother, Sara, move to a DP camp in Feldafing, Germany. The three remain there for five years.
- Ben Helfgott comes to England as one of "The Boys."
- August 26 Norbert Wollheim: "We have been saved, but we are not liberated." He champions the cause of displaced persons and will be elected vice-chairman of the Central Committee of Liberated Jews in the British Zone in Germany.

1946

- Roman and Leon Kniker (Kent) arrive in New York. They are sent to live in a home in Atlanta, Georgia.
- February 27 Abraham Sutzkever testifies at the Nuremberg trials.

- May 24   Vladka and Benjamin Meed arrive in the United States and soon start their work with the survivor community.
- September   Hirsch Vasser helps uncover ten tin boxes containing thousands of documents from the Oyneg Shabes Archive.

1947

- Abraham and Freydke Sutzkever immigrate to Palestine. He writes and promotes Yiddish poetry in the land that will soon be called Israel.
- Norbert Wollheim serves as a witness in the 1947 I. G. Farben trial.
- Chiune Sugihara and his family arrive back in Japan. Several months later he is asked to resign from the Foreign Ministry.
- Anne Frank's diary is published.
- Henia and Ilona Karmel's poems are published as *Songs from Behind the Barbed Wire* while the sisters are still hospitalized in Sweden.
- Fritz Westfeld, now Fred Westfield, enters Vanderbilt University in Nashville.
- Tousia Goldberg (Tess Wise) immigrates to the United States and comes to Orlando, Florida. Decades later she will establish the first Holocaust museum and education center in the Southeast.

1948

- In New York Vladka Meed publishes *On Both Sides of the Wall*, one of the earliest accounts of the Warsaw Ghetto Uprising.
- Henia (Karmel) and her husband, Leon Wolfe, move to New York.
- Leibke Kaganowicz, now Leon Kahn, immigrates to Canada.

1949

- Ilona Karmel moves to New York. She will later serve as a lecturer in creative writing at MIT.
- Chanka Garfinkel (Helen Greenspun) and her siblings immigrate to the United States.
- Chava Rosenfarb marries, and the couple immigrates to Canada, where she continues to write.

1950

- Polish construction workers find two big milk cans containing thousands of documents from the Oyneg Shabes Archive.
- Nesse and Jack Godin and Nesse's mother immigrate to America, settling in the Washington, DC, area.

1951

- Norbert Wollheim sues I. G. Farben in Frankfurt Regional Court for compensation as a slave laborer. In September he leaves to reside in the United States.

1953

- Norbert Wollheim wins the lawsuit against I. G. Farben for compensation as a slave laborer at the industrial plant at Buna/Monowitz, setting the precedent for other slave laborers to be paid.

1956

- Ben Helfgott, formerly a prisoner at Terezin, is captain of the British Olympic Weightlifting Team. He also serves as captain in 1960.

1960

- Peter Malkin and the Israeli Mossad team capture Adolf Eichmann in Buenos Aires, Argentina, and take him to Israel to stand trial.

Deborah Romm of the Romm Press in Vilna, circa 1900

Note About the Typeface for the Hebrew Word *Zachor*

The typeface known as Vilna font, which is used to write the Hebrew word *zachor*, was created by the Romm (or Rom) Press, a major publishing house and printing press known for its editions of traditional Jewish texts such as the Babylonian Talmud. This font was a distinctive trademark of the Romm Press, an institution that helped Vilna earn its reputation as the Jerusalem of Lithuania. The font is still used today.

The Romm Press in Vilna

Herman Lodinger

Acknowledgments

(Ghazal of Thank-Yous*)*

Dad, Herman Lodinger, bombardier in the air,
Began marching the brave in my head to this end

Martha, then Jerry and Lynn at the start,
Revise with new eyes and pen red toward this end

Morry in purple writes poems that inspire
Since college he drives me ahead for this end

Elaine cries "Write on," show lifeblood and breath
Al Rocheleau reads the unsaid in each end

Marianne measures the book as it grows
So teachers and students are fed in the end

Gabrielle poses poems sewn in hems
Maxine finds life, not dread, in the end

Mitchell knows history (a scholar and friend)
Ken watches so no one's misled in the end

The Yiddish Book Center reviews and amends
Catherine cites "Sutzkever said" in the end

Elaine Laegeler's language eye tends to each word
Under her care and stead there's an end

Paul knows he will find me buried in books
I'm lucky that we are still wed at the end

Joel, on the keyboard, teaches with skill
He schools me so verse can be read in the end

Byron by sketching makes names come to life
Wholly sensing their spirit instead of their end

The women protestors rest in my heart—
And Norbert, Petr, and Fred in the end

I wish to thank the individuals who shared their stories and read my work to ensure that it artistically and accurately reflects their experiences. Dr. Fred Westfield initially said that he could not imagine poetry about the *Kindertransport* but, after reading, wrote that the poems became pictures that moved him and stirred his memories. Polish survivors Helen Greenspun and scholar-educator Tess Wise enthusiastically supported poetic retellings of Holocaust experiences. Roman Kent expressed how much the tribute meant to him. It was a privilege to meet Father Patrick Desbois and to present him with the poem that honors him. I am indebted to Vladka Meed of blessed memory for allowing me to study the Holocaust on a trip of monumental importance to me. I hope that she would have been pleased with the book that is the fruit of our time together.

Writing a book of poetry, history, and illustrations has required support from a team of individuals of many talents. Poetry was the fuse for the book, and Al Rocheleau, a poet, my teacher, and a wizard of syntax, semantics, and sound, has guided me in his intensive Twelve Chairs Advanced Poetry Course in Orlando, Florida, over the past several years. As a poet, professor, and president of the Gwendolyn Brooks Writers Association of Florida, Dr. Stephen Caldwell Wright has lent his voice to support the power of verse to tell these vital stories.

Fellow teachers helped me know that this book would find a place in the hearts of students and the general public. Elaine Laegeler has read and reread every word and has been incredibly generous with her time and skills. Dr. Harriet Sepinwall of the College of Saint Elizabeth has inspired me with her extensive knowledge of teaching the Holocaust. From Vermont, master teacher Marianne Doe read the work as it evolved and made valuable suggestions along the way. The late David Erdmann, dean of Rollins College, knew the power of poetry and encouraged me to keep these stories alive. Also from Rollins, Dr. Rick Bommelje, the "Listening Doctor," offered guidance for sharing these stories.

Scholars have checked facts and contributed their expertise. After relying on countless reference books by Dr. Michael

Berenbaum, I was deeply honored that he read my manuscript with discerning eyes and fine-tuned details and nuance. Mitchell Bloomer, educator par excellence at the Holocaust Memorial Resource and Education Center of Florida and fellow classmate from our 1991 educators' trip, has measured all poems and histories, applying his sensitivity and extensive knowledge. Mrs. Tess Wise, the founder of this same Holocaust resource center and pioneer in Holocaust education, contributed her insights and encouragement. From the University of Central Florida, Kenneth L. Hanson, PhD, Director of the Judaic Studies Program, has been a reader and cheerleader for this book since its early stages and has incorporated my poems into his online class on the history of the Holocaust. Dr. Marty Manor Mullins used many of the poems in her "Holocaust in Literature and Film" class at Tulane University in 2014.

From research centers around the world, help has come forth. Ephraim Kaye, director of the International Seminars at the International School for Holocaust Studies at Yad Vashem in Jerusalem, and reference librarians and project directors at the United States Holocaust Memorial Museum in Washington, DC, answered questions when my usual resources did not suffice. The Tennessee Holocaust Commission in Nashville supplied additional information about the *Kindertransport* experience of Vanderbilt professor Dr. Fred Westfield. Special thanks go to Catherine Madsen, bibliographer at the Yiddish Book Center in Amherst, Massachusetts, for her frequent and authoritative responses over the past few years. Jonathan Brent and Lyudmila Sholokhova at the YIVO Institute in New York answered questions about Abraham Sutzkever. The Holocaust Educational Trust in London was helpful in confirming details about Ben Helfgott and in providing a way for him to read my work. The Jewish Foundation for the Righteous in New York, particularly Stanlee J. Stahl, was similarly helpful regarding Roman Kent. Finally, a note of thanks goes to Dr. Joshua Colwell, a planetary scientist and professor of physics at the University of Central Florida, for checking the astronomy terms in the Petr Ginz poem—an unusual pairing of our respective fields.

On a local level, I wish to thank Winter Park Public Library Interlibrary Loan Coordinator Jeanna Wong and Librarian Cherilyn Taylor for procuring countless books over the past five years. Ellen Schellhause and her staff at the Maitland Public Library were always ready to help. The entire staff of the Holocaust Memorial Resource and Education Center of Florida has lent constant support. Dr. Hansmartin Hertlein graciously answered both simple and more complex questions involving the German language.

The early architects of this book include experienced critical readers: Martha Williamson, Dr. Gerald Schiffhorst, Lynn Schiffhorst, and Dr. Maxine Goldberg. Elaine Person and the other poets in the Twelve Chairs program offered critiques as they listened to poems read in class. Gabrielle Bennett, a fellow writer, still talks about the Karmel sisters, who hid their poems inside the hems of their dresses. Dr. Morry Edwards, a poet, psychologist, and friend since our student days at Vanderbilt University, has furnished a lifetime of inspiration.

The builders of this book for its journey home have worked diligently to weave various textures into a unified tapestry. Again, I highlight Elaine Laegeler, who helped me on a regular basis to create a book that reflects deep-seated respect for each individual. Dr. Art Cross, Nancy-Lee and John Thompson, Shannon Gridley, Karen James, Reverend Danielle Morris, Ruth Titus, Linda Clark, Rebekah Todiah, Jeffrey Byrd, Dr. Philip M. Smith, and Linda Fessel read with insight and sensitivity. Max Reed shared her decades of experience as an editor to draft a well-constructed book, and copy editor Mary Beth Constant balanced the requisite consistency and predictability of form with the freshness and fire of ideas, words, and images. Lucie Winborne read with the eyes of a proofreader and the ear of the poet. I thank Rick Kilby for designing the perfect cover and Matt Peters for providing valuable publishing advice.

My family has been my sanctuary and my center. My husband, Paul, has shared the importance of this project from its inception to the present. I particularly appreciate his lawyerly attention to detail with the maps, list of references, and timeline. My son, Joel, patiently taught me new computer skills, provided thoughtful technical support, and has served as a sample reader and sounding board for five years. My daughter, Gail VanMatre, helped with artistic details, and Sharon Hildebrand, my sister, prepared the illustrations for display at museums and galleries. My most longstanding debt goes to my parents for their constant faith that I could tell the stories, first of my dad's experiences as a POW and then of the individuals whom he tried to save when he enlisted in the US Army Eighth Air Force.

Finally, my deepest thanks go to Byron Marshall, who has illustrated this book with his heart, soul, intelligence, and creativity. After he attended my talk about Jewish resistance during the Holocaust, Byron was first in line to ask questions about Petr Ginz, the gifted young man from Prague. He devoured the references I sent him, and several weeks later we met to talk about Petr Ginz. When he showed me his sketch of Petr, I immediately asked if he would consider illustrating my book. Without hesitation he said that he would be honored to be part of such a project. While I flooded him with history, poetry, and hundreds of photographs, he balanced these images with his vast storehouse of knowledge to render illustrations that are both rooted in history yet highly original. It has been a privilege to work with such a talented artist who fleshed out my vision in a more beautiful way than I could have imagined.

REFERENCES

Through Leaden Cloud

Durand, Arthur A. *Stalag Luft III: The Secret Story.* Baton Rouge: Louisiana State University Press, 1988.

458th Bombardment Group (H). "Crew 20 - Assigned 753rd Squadron - October 1943." http://www.458bg.com/crew20lamb.htm.

Mandelkern, Holly Lodinger. "Wheels of War." In *My Wheels*, Florida Writers Association Collection, vol. 4, 125–128. Sarasota, FL: Peppertree Press, 2012.

DEPARTURES

Heartbeats

Anne Frank Stichting (Anne Frank Foundation). *Anne Frank in the World.* 3rd rev. ed. Amsterdam: Uitgeverij Bert Bakker, 1985.

van der Rol, Ruud, and Rian Verhoeven, in association with the Anne Frank House. *Anne Frank, Beyond the Diary: A Photographic Remembrance.* Translated by Tony Langham and Plym Peters. New York: Viking, 1993.

The Small World of Little Fritz
Watching Myself Watch My Son
Crosscurrents
I Am That Child
Transported

Harris, Mark Jonathan, and Deborah Oppenheimer.
Into the Arms of Strangers: Stories of the Kindertransport.
London: Bloomsbury, 2000.

Into the Arms of Strangers: Stories of the Kindertransport,
DVD. Written and directed by Mark Jonathan Harris.
Warner Bros., 2001.

Kaplan, Marion A. *Between Dignity and Despair: Jewish Life
in Nazi Germany.* New York: Oxford University Press,
1998.

"Kindertransport." *The Reunion,* hosted by Sue MacGregor.
BBC Radio 4, September 12, 2010. http://www.bbc.
co.uk/programmes/b00tnjsx.

Kindertransport Association. "Life in Britain." http://
Kindertransport.org/history04_Britain.htm.

Müller, Melissa, and Monika Tatzkow. *Lost Lives, Lost Art:
Jewish Collectors, Nazi Art Theft, and the Quest for Justice.*
New York: Vendome Press, 2010.

Prest, David. "Evacuees in World War Two - The True
Story." BBC. Last updated February 17, 2011. http://
bbc.co.uk/history/british/Britain_wwtwo/evacuees_01.
shtml.

Robbins, Lisa. "In the Face of Destruction." *Vanderbilt Magazine*, Spring 2008, 44–53.

Tennessee Holocaust Commission. *Living On: Portraits of Tennessee Survivors and Liberators.* Knoxville: University of Tennessee Press, 2008.

Westfield, Fred. Interview by Felicia Anchor, Interview Code 28538, USC Shoah Foundation, April 25, 1997. Los Angeles: University of Southern California.

A Place for Us?

Block, Gay, and Malka Drucker. *Rescuers: Portraits of Moral Courage in the Holocaust.* New York: Holmes and Meier, 1992.

de Waal, Edmund. *The Hare with Amber Eyes: A Family's Century of Art and Loss.* New York: Farrar, Straus and Giroux, 2010.

Goldberger, Leo, ed. *The Rescue of the Danish Jews: Moral Courage Under Stress.* New York: New York University Press, 1987.

Klarsfeld, Serge. Keynote Yom HaShoah Address. Roth Jewish Community Center of Greater Orlando (Maitland, Florida), April 18, 1999.

Richarz, Monika, ed. *Jewish Life in Germany: Memoirs from Three Centuries.* Translated by Stella P. Rosenfeld and Sidney Rosenfeld. Bloomington: Indiana University Press, 1991.

Rosbottom, Ronald C. *When Paris Went Dark: The City of Light Under German Occupation, 1940–1944.* New York: Little, Brown, 2014.

Vishniac, Roman. *Polish Jews: A Pictorial Record.* New York: Schocken Books, 1947.

Weapons of the Spirit, VHS. Written, produced, and directed by Pierre Sauvage. Pierre Sauvage Productions and Friends of Le Chambon Inc., 1988.

Zuccotti, Susan. *The Holocaust, the French, and the Jews.* New York: Basic Books, 1993.

Packing Her Bag
Watching My Daughter Pack Her Bag

Adelson, Alan, and Robert Lapides, eds. *Łódź Ghetto: Inside a Community under Siege.* New York: Viking Penguin, 1991.

Goldsmith, Martin. *The Inextinguishable Symphony: A True Story of Music and Love in Nazi Germany.* New York: John Wiley & Sons, 2000.

Holocaust Education & Archive Research Team. "Frankfurt am Main: The City and the Holocaust." http://www.holocaustresearchproject.org/nazioccupation/frankfurt.html.

International Institute for Holocaust Research, Yad Vashem. "Deportation Database and Research Project Online Guide: Germany." http://www.yadvashem.org/yv/en/about/institute/deportations_catalog_details.asp?country=GERMANY.

Kaplan, Marion A. *Between Dignity and Despair: Jewish Life in Nazi Germany.* New York: Oxford University Press, 1998.

Richarz, Monika, ed. *Jewish Life in Germany: Memoirs from Three Centuries.* Translated by Stella P. Rosenfeld and Sidney Rosenfeld. Bloomington: Indiana University Press, 1991.

PRAYING IN PENCIL

Between the Lines

Beit Theresienstadt. "The Collections." http://www. bterezin.org.il/120869/the-collections.

Brown, Jean E., Elaine C. Stephens, and Janet E. Rubin, eds. *Images from the Holocaust: A Literature Anthology.* Lincolnwood, IL: National Textbook Company, 1997.

"Chava Rosenfarb: Biography," on the official website of the late poet. http://chavarosenfarb.com/biography.

Groag, Trude. *Poems by a Compassionate Nurse.* Givat Haim Ihud, Israel: Beit Theresienstadt, 1975.

Inbar, Yehudit. *Spots of Light: To Be a Woman in the Holocaust.* Jerusalem: Yad Vashem, 2007.

Karmel, Henia, and Ilona Karmel. *A Wall of Two: Poems of Resistance and Suffering from Kraków to Buchenwald and Beyond.* Berkeley: University of California Press, 2007.

Krick-Aigner, Kirsten. "Gertrud Kolmar." In *Jewish Women: A Comprehensive Historical Encyclopedia*. Jewish Women's Archive. http://www.jwa.org/encyclopedia/article/kolmar-gertrud.

Langer, Lawrence L., ed. *Art from the Ashes: A Holocaust Anthology*. New York: Oxford University Press, 1995.

Morgentaler, Goldie. "Chava Rosenfarb." In *Jewish Women: A Comprehensive Historical Encyclopedia*. Jewish Women's Archive. http://www.jwa.org/encyclopedia/article/rosenfarb-chava.

Newman, Richard, with Karen Kirtley. *Alma Rosé: Vienna to Auschwitz*. Portland, OR: Amadeus Press, 2000.

Ofer, Dalia, and Lenore J. Weitzman, eds. *Women in the Holocaust*. New Haven, CT: Yale University Press, 1998.

Poetry in Hell: Warsaw Ghetto Poems from the Ringelblum Archives. Translated by Sarah Traister Moskovitz, foreword by Michael Berenbaum. http://poetryinhell.org/.

Sachs, Nelly. *O the Chimneys: Selected Poems, Including Eli, a Verse Play*. New York: Farrar, Straus and Giroux, 1967.

Senesh, Hannah. *Hannah Senesh: Her Life and Diary, The First Complete Edition*. Woodstock, VT: Jewish Lights Publishing, 2007.

Spies, Gerty. *My Years in Theresienstadt: How One Woman Survived the Holocaust*. Translated by Jutta R. Tragnitz. Amherst, NY: Prometheus Books, 1997.

Teichman, Milton, and Sharon Leder, eds. *Truth and Lamentation: Stories and Poems on the Holocaust.* Urbana: University of Illinois Press, 1994.

Parallel Limbs
You Never Saw Another Butterfly

Frank, Anne. *The Diary of a Young Girl: The Critical Edition.* New York: Doubleday, 1989.

Volavková, Hana, ed. *I Never Saw Another Butterfly: Children's Drawings and Poems from Terezin Concentration Camp, 1942–1944.* New York: Schocken, 1993.

Overdue: Book Reports, May–September 1944
Lines in Space

Ginz, Petr. "Linocuts." *Vedem*, 1943.

———. *The Diary of Petr Ginz: 1941–1942.* Edited by Chava Pressburger. New York: Atlantic Monthly Press, 2007.

Intrator, Miriam. "Avenues of Intellectual Resistance in the Ghetto Theresienstadt: Escape Through the Central Library, Books, and Reading." *Libri* 54 (2004): 237–246.

Křížková, Marie Rút, Kurt Jiří Kotouč, and Zdeněk Ornest, eds. *We Are Children Just the Same: Vedem, the Secret Magazine by the Boys of Terezín.* Philadelphia: Jewish Publication Society, 1995.

Mais, Yitzchak, ed. *Daring to Resist: Jewish Defiance in the Holocaust.* New York: Museum of Jewish Heritage, 2007.

Music of Remembrance. "*Vedem* Educator's Guide." http://
www.musicofremembrance.org/~musicofr/sites/default/
files/upload/*Vedem*_Teacher_Guide.pdf.

Owen, Tina. "The Last Flight of Petr Ginz." *Iowa Alumni
Magazine* (April 2013). http://www.iowalum.com/
magazine/apr13/lastflight.cfm?page=all.

Rappaport, Doreen. *Beyond Courage: The Untold Story of
Jewish Resistance During the Holocaust.* Somerville, MA:
Candlewick Press, 2012.

Verne, Jules. *From the Earth to the Moon.* Translated by
Lowell Bair. New York: Bantam, 1967.

Zapruder, Alexandra, ed. *Salvaged Pages: Young Writers'
Diaries of the Holocaust.* New Haven, CT: Yale University
Press, 2002.

So the World Would Know

Kassow, Samuel D. "A Stone Under History's Wheel."
Pakn Treger 43 (Fall 2003): 14–23.

———. *Who Will Write Our History?: Emanuel Ringelblum,
the Warsaw Ghetto, and the Oyneg Shabes Archive.*
Bloomington: Indiana University Press, 2007.

Ringelblum, Emmanuel. *Notes from the Warsaw Ghetto: The
Journal of Emmanuel Ringelblum.* Edited and translated by
Jacob Sloan. 1956. Reprint, New York: Schocken, 1974.

STANDING IN BLOOD

Bowl of Soup

Adelson, Alan, and Robert Lapides, eds. *Łódź Ghetto: Inside a Community under Siege.* New York: Viking Penguin, 1991.

Grossman, Mendel. *With a Camera in the Ghetto.* New York: Schocken, 1977.

Kaplan, Chaim. *Scroll of Agony: The Warsaw Diary of Chaim A. Kaplan.* Bloomington: Indiana University Press, 1999.

Zapruder, Alexandra, ed. *Salvaged Pages: Young Writers' Diaries of the Holocaust.* New Haven, CT: Yale University Press, 2002.

His Overtures of Love

Ackerman, Diane. *The Zookeeper's Wife.* New York: W. W. Norton, 2007.

Korczak, Janusz. *Ghetto Diary.* 1978. Reprint, New Haven, CT: Yale University Press, 2003.

Lifton, Betty Jean. *The King of Children: A Biography of Janusz Korczak.* New York: Farrar, Straus and Giroux, 1988.

Timing Is Everything
History Lessons

Meed, Vladka. Interview by Linda Kuzmack, call number RG–50.030*0153, June 19, 1991. Washington, DC: United States Holocaust Memorial Museum.

———. Interview by Renee Firestone, Interview Code 15197, USC Shoah Foundation, May 15, 1996. Los Angeles: University of Southern California.

———. *On Both Sides of the Wall: Memoirs from the Warsaw Ghetto.* Washington, DC: Holocaust Library, 1993.

Chanka Garfinkel: Guarding the Memories
Telltale Lines

Greenspun, Helen. Interview Code 19330, USC Shoah Foundation, September 5, 1996. Los Angeles: University of Southern California.

Hagstrom, Suzan E. *Sara's Children and the Destruction of Chmielnik.* Spotsylvania, VA: Sergeant Kirkland's Press, 2001.

Standing Prayer
No Art

Harris, Mark Jonathan, and Deborah Oppenheimer. *Into the Arms of Strangers: Stories of the Kindertransport.* London: Bloomsbury, 2000.

Wollheim Memorial. Official website of the memorial at Goethe University. www.wollheim-memorial.de.

Wollheim, Norbert. Interview by Linda Kuzmack, call number RG–50.030*0257, May 10, 1991, and May 17, 1991. Washington, DC: United States Holocaust Memorial Museum.

———. Interview by Sandra Bradley, call number RG–50.042*0032, February 18, 1992. Washington, DC: United States Holocaust Memorial Museum.

Patzan

Eliach, Yaffa. *There Once Was a World.* Boston: Little, Brown, 1998.

Kahn, Leon. *No Time to Mourn: The True Story of a Jewish Partisan Fighter.* Vancouver, BC: Ronsdale, 2004.

Unlikely Heroes, DVD. Directed by Richard Trank. Los Angeles: Moriah Films of the Simon Wiesenthal Center, 2006.

Yoran, Shalom. *The Defiant: A True Story.* New York: St. Martin's Press, 1996.

"Unter dayne vayse shtern": A Sonnet for Sutzkever Sutzkever's Stars

Kramer, Aaron, ed. and trans. *The Last Lullaby: Poetry from the Holocaust.* Syracuse, NY: Syracuse University Press, 1998.

Kruk, Herman. *The Last Days of the Jerusalem of Lithuania: Chronicles from the Vilna Ghetto and Camps, 1939–1944.* Edited by Benjamin Harshav and translated by Barbara Harshav. New Haven, CT: YIVO Institute for Jewish Research, 2002.

Langer, Lawrence, ed. *Art from the Ashes: A Holocaust Anthology.* New York: Oxford University Press, 1995.

Sutzkever, Abraham. *A. Sutzkever: Selected Poetry and Prose.* Translated by Barbara Harshav and Benjamin Harshav. Berkeley: University of California Press, 1991.

———. "Unter dayne vayse shtern." In *Lider fun yam ha-moves: fun Vilner geto, vald, un vander.* Tel-Aviv: Farlag Bergen-Belzen, 1968.

L'Chaim

Godin, Nesse. "Mama Picking My Husband, Jack." In *Echoes of Memory*, vol. 6, edited by Margaret Peterson and United States Holocaust Memorial Museum, 15. Washington, DC: United States Holocaust Memorial Museum, 2011. http://www.ushmm.org/remember/office-of-survivor-affairs/memory-project.

———. Testimony. Resources for Educators: Online Workshop. Washington, DC: United States Holocaust Memorial Museum, n.d. http://www.ushmm.org/educators/online-workshop/personal-testimony/introduction.

A Glezele Tei

Wise, Tess. Interview by Susan Rosenblum, Interview
Code 19225, USC Shoah Foundation, September 9,
1996. Los Angeles: University of Southern California.

RESCUE

Mr. Sugihara's Eyes

Gilbert, Martin. *The Righteous: The Unsung Heroes of the
Holocaust.* New York: Henry Holt, 2003.

Mochizuki, Ken. *Passage to Freedom: The Sugihara Story.*
Afterword by Hiroki Sugihara. New York: Lee & Low
Books, 1997.

Poser, Bill. "Chiune Sugihara." *Language Log* (blog), May
7, 2005. http:// itre.cis.upenn.edu/~myl/languagelog/
archives/002136.html.

"Sugihara: Conspiracy of Kindness." Website for the
documentary *Sugihara: Conspiracy of Kindness*, directed
by Robert Kirk, PBS, 2005.
http://www.pbs.org/wgbh/sugihara/index.html.

United States Holocaust Memorial Museum. "Flight
and Rescue" (online exhibit). http://www.ushmm.org/
exhibition/flight-rescue/.

Visas for Life Foundation. http://www.visasforlife.org/

Kissing the Wall

Gilbert, Martin. *The Righteous: The Unsung Heroes of the Holocaust.* New York: Henry Holt, 2003.

Greenfeld, Howard. *The Hidden Children.* New York: Ticknor & Fields, 1993.

Gutman, Israel, ed. *The Encyclopedia of the Righteous Among the Nations: Rescuers of Jews During the Holocaust.* Jerusalem: Yad Vashem, 2003–2007.

Paldiel, Mordecai. *The Path of the Righteous: Gentile Rescuers of Jews During the Holocaust.* Hoboken, NJ: Ktav, 1993.

Singer, Flora. "I Did It!" In *Echoes of Memory*, vol. 2, edited by Margaret Peterson and United States Holocaust Memorial Museum, 63–65. Washington, DC: United States Holocaust Memorial Museum, 2004. http://www.ushmm.org/remember/office-of-survivor-affairs/memory-project.

———. Testimony, *First Person* series. Washington, DC: United States Holocaust Memorial Museum, 2003. http://www.ushmm.org/remember/office-of-survivor-affairs/survivor-volunteer/flora-singer.

The Likeness of a Man

Borden, Louise. *His Name Was Raoul Wallenberg: Courage, Rescue, and Mystery During World War II.* Boston: Houghton Mifflin Harcourt, 2012.

Gilbert, Martin. *The Righteous: The Unsung Heroes of the Holocaust.* New York: Henry Holt, 2003.

Paldiel, Mordecai. *The Path of the Righteous: Gentile Rescuers of Jews During the Holocaust.* Hoboken, NJ: Ktav, 1993.

Wallenberg, Raoul. *Letters and Dispatches, 1924–1944.* Translated by Kjersti Board. New York: Arcade, 1995.

A Crowd of Hosts

Gilbert, Martin. *The Righteous: The Unsung Heroes of the Holocaust.* New York: Henry Holt, 2003.

Risen and Rescued

Nathan, Joan. *Jewish Cooking in America.* New York: Alfred A. Knopf, 1994.

ROUNDUPS

Uprooted

Adelson, Alan, and Robert Lapides, eds. *Łódź Ghetto: Inside a Community under Siege.* New York: Viking Penguin, 1991.

Kent, Roman. *Courage Was My Only Option: The Autobiography of Roman Kent.* New York: Vantage Press, 2008.

———. Interview by Benjamin Weiner, Interview Code 14613, USC Shoah Foundation, April 29, 1996. Los Angeles: University of Southern California.

———. *My Dog Lala: The Touching True Story of a Young Boy and His Dog During the Holocaust.* Auburn Hills, MI: Teacher's Discovery, 2006.

Sierakowiak, Dawid. *The Diary of Dawid Sierakowiak: Five Notebooks from the Łódź Ghetto.* New York: Oxford University Press, 1996.

YIVO Institute for Jewish Research. *Guide to the Records of the Nachman Zonabend Collection, 1939–1944,* RG 241, Folder #181, Item #36. Processed by Marek Web. New York: YIVO Institute for Jewish Research, 2004. http://findingaids.cjh.org/?pID=109126.

Feathers

Epstein, David. "The Strength to Carry On." *Sports Illustrated,* July 9–16, 2012, 97–101.

Gilbert, Martin. *The Boys: The Untold Story of 732 Young Concentration Camp Survivors.* New York: Henry Holt, 1996.

Holocaust Education & Archive Research Team. "Mendel Grossman: The Łódź Ghetto Photographer." http://www.holocaustresearchproject.org/ghettos/grossman.html.

Kaplan, Marion A. *Between Dignity and Despair: Jewish Life in Nazi Germany.* New York: Oxford University Press, 1998.

The Witness Stands

Auschwitz-Birkenau Memorial and Museum. "The Death of Silent Witnesses to History." News release, March 27, 2007. http://auschwitz.org/en/museum/news/the-death-of-silent-witnesses-to-history,466.html.

Desbois, Father Patrick. *The Holocaust by Bullets: A Priest's Journey to Uncover the Truth Behind the Murder of 1.5 Million Jews.* New York: Palgrave Macmillan, 2008.

Escape from Sobibór, DVD. Directed by Jack Gold. Unicorn Video, 2002.

Frank, Anne. *The Diary of a Young Girl: The Critical Edition.* New York: Doubleday, 1989.

Jewish Partisan Educational Foundation. "Study Guide: Tuvia Bielski: Rescue is Resistance." http://www.jewishpartisans.org/pdfs/Tuvia_Bielski_Study_Guide.pdf.

Kaplan, Chaim. *Scroll of Agony: The Warsaw Diary of Chaim A. Kaplan.* Bloomington: Indiana University Press, 1999.

Mais, Yitzchak, ed. *Daring to Resist: Jewish Defiance in the Holocaust.* New York: Museum of Jewish Heritage, 2007.

Singer, Flora. Testimony, *First Person* series. Washington, DC: United States Holocaust Memorial Museum, 2003. http://www.ushmm.org/remember/office-of-survivor-affairs/survivor-volunteer/flora-singer.

Tec, Nechama. *Defiance: The Bielski Partisans.* New York: Oxford University Press, 1993.

Memories in Color

Baskin, Neal. *Hunting Eichmann: How a Band of Survivors and a Young Spy Agency Chased Down the World's Most Notorious Nazi.* Boston: Houghton Mifflin Harcourt, 2009.

Malkin, Peter Z. *The Argentina Journal.* New York: VWF Publishing, 2002.

Malkin, Peter Z., and Harry Stein. *Eichmann in My Hands.* New York: Warner Books, 1990.

Misericordia for the Last Jews of Busk, Ukraine

Desbois, Father Patrick. *The Holocaust by Bullets: A Priest's Journey to Uncover the Truth Behind the Murder of 1.5 Million Jews.* New York: Palgrave Macmillan, 2008.

Sciolino, Elaine. "A Priest Methodically Reveals Ukrainian Jews' Fate." *New York Times*, October 5, 2007. http://www.nytimes.com/2007/10/05/world/europe/05iht-profile.3.7770027.html.

Shayari, Abraham (formerly Abraham Karawan). "A History of the Town of Busk." http://edwebproject.org/busk.html.

Voices on Antisemitism (podcast). Father Patrick Desbois with Daniel Greene. United States Holocaust Memorial Museum, November 8, 2007. http://www.ushmm.org/confront-antisemitism/antisemitism-podcast/father-patrick-desbois.

GENERAL REFERENCES

Berenbaum, Michael. *The World Must Know: The History of the Holocaust as Told in the United States Holocaust Memorial Museum.* Boston: Little, Brown, 1993.

Gilbert, Martin. *Atlas of the Holocaust.* New York: William Morrow, 1993.

Hogan, David J., editor-in-chief. *The Holocaust Chronicle: A History in Words and Pictures.* Lincolnwood, IL: Publications International, 2003.

Rappaport, Doreen. *Beyond Courage: The Untold Story of Jewish Resistance During the Holocaust.* Somerville, MA: Candlewick Press, 2012.

About the Illustrator

Byron Marshall is an artist and illustrator in Central Florida. He counts Chagall and Bakst as influences and is happy to walk in the inky footsteps of Arthur Rackham and Edward Ardizonne.

He can be reached at byron@ByronIllustrator.com.

For more information, go to ByronIllustrator.com

About the Author

Macbeth Studio

Holly Mandelkern is a poet, Holocaust educator, and lecturer. After studying with other teachers at Yad Vashem, she taught for twenty years at the Summer Teachers' Institute at the Holocaust Memorial Resource and Education Center of Florida. A recipient of the Thomas Burnett Swann Poetry Prize for 2016, she is a 2015 graduate of the Twelve Chairs Advanced Poetry Workshop. Her work has appeared in journals of the National Council of Teachers of English, the Gwendolyn Brooks Writers Association of Florida, and the Florida State Poets Association. Her most recent Holocaust poems appeared in *Prism* Spring 2016.

She lives in Winter Park, Florida, and can be reached at hollymandelkern@gmail.com.

For more information, go to HollyMandelkern.com.

CPSIA information can be obtained
at www.ICGtesting.com
Printed in the USA
LVOW01s0246170317
527536LV00002B/2/P

9 780998 498904